T0405391

MYSTICAL REALM
TAROT

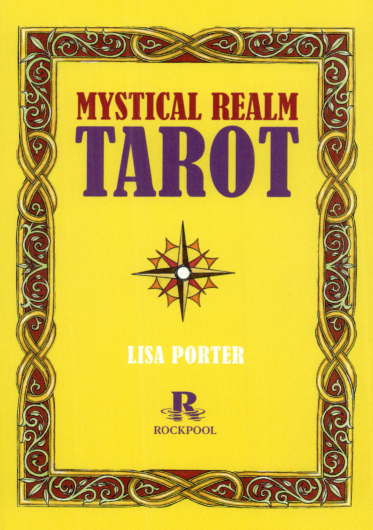

MYSTICAL REALM
TAROT

LISA PORTER

ROCKPOOL

A Rockpool book
PO Box 252
Summer Hill NSW 2130
Australia

rockpoolpublishing.com
Follow us! **f** ⭕ rockpoolpublishing
Tag your images with #rockpoolpublishing

Published in 2022 by Rockpool Publishing

ISBN: 9781925946567

Edited by Brooke Halliwell
Design and typesetting by Sara Lindberg, Rockpool Publishing

Printed and bound in China
10 9 8 7 6 5 4 3 2 1

CONTENTS

MINOR ARCANA

INTRODUCTION

BRIEF HISTORICAL OVERVIEW
OF TAROT CARD ORIGINS

The exact origins of the tarot deck are somewhat debatable. A lot of specific information is, to this very day, still shrouded in mystery. However, most agree they originated in Northern Italy during the 14th or early 15th century.

The oldest-known surviving deck is the Visconti-Sforza deck, which dates to around 1440. What remains of these decks are fragmented. There are 26 cards at the Accademia Carrara and 35 at the Morgan Library & Museum in New York. The rest are in private collections. To date The Tower, The Devil, Three of Swords and Knight of Coins are missing.

Tarocchi (Trifoni/Trumps) was the original popular game the deck was used for.

By the 18th century tarot decks were being arranged for divination and occult purposes. Cartomancy with the tarot became fashionable with the Italian and French nobility, and later the practice spread all throughout Europe.

With the fascination of the card divination spread, the readings and designs of the cards became more elaborate, refined, insightful and complex.

Antoine Court De Gébelin, who was trained for priesthood, published a detailed analysis of the tarot deck in 1781. In this, he explained how tarot deck symbolism originated from the mysticism of Egyptian high priests. He was also convinced he found esoteric yet anecdotal correlations with tarot and the Hebrew mysticism of Kabbalah and tree of life.

By 1909 the Rider-Waite deck, drawn by Pamela Colman Smith and directed by Arthur Edward Waite, was published. This brilliant deck popularised and conceptually transformed the tarot deck for 20th-century culture. Both Waite and Colman Smith were members of the Hermetic Order of the Golden Dawn.

Today the Rider-Waite tarot deck is still widely used and considered an excellent blueprint archetypal template of esoteric divination information for the journey of life.

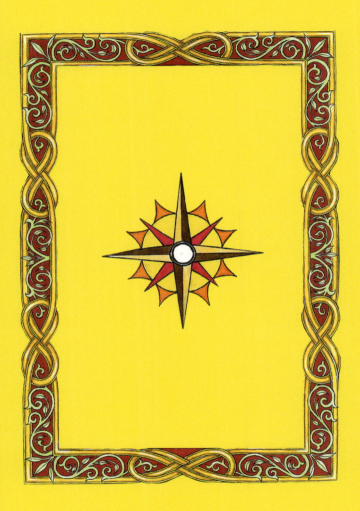

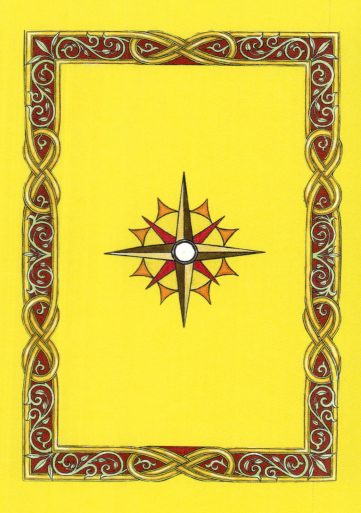

ABOUT THE *MYSTICAL REALM TAROT* DECK

I imagined, illustrated and authored this deck. It is the third deck I have created that has been published, the first being *Journey to the Goddess Realm*, the second being *Mystic Martians* and now this third *Mystical Realm Tarot*.

All through this creation I have deliberately stayed as close, symbolically, to the Rider-Waite tarot deck's general format and paradigm. I believe the Rider-Waite tarot is the perfect symbolic iconography to subconsciously use as an esoteric reference of exploration into The Fool's Journey, discovering all the different necessary stages required for integrating wisdom, wholeness and individual growth.

Even though the *Mystical Realm Tarot* deck is slightly altered from traditional tarot decks, I never wanted to wander too far from the traditional occultic, archetypal and symbolic messages for there is endless material hidden within, depending on the reader's multi-layered level of awareness. Also, I feel mixed messages can sometimes be confusing to the enquirer if the images are too different. I also wanted to pay homage to the great and original Rider-Waite tarot deck, for it taught me much in my younger years and even to this day I find it to be a highly credible deck.

I have creatively given a new visual content to the cards without convoluting the original meaning.

The *Mystical Realm Tarot* deck typically holds 74 cartomancy cards – 22 Major Arcana cards and 52 Minor Arcana cards of divination.

The Major Arcana tarot cards symbolise the far more complex hidden themes, long-term karmic lessons and larger hidden topics regarding the query. These major cards are saying there are consciousness-expanding lessons, bigger than what is even within the question, that pertains to the enquirer. These bigger questions will overlap into many areas of the individual's life journey.

Even though the Minor Arcana cards can and often do have a big impact in this third-dimensional realm, the Major Arcana cards hold key archetypal forces that are networked into higher realms of awareness and therefore hold far larger patterns of expanded consciousness. And hence, far higher lessons with consequential far higher dharma.

This, however, does not take away from the importance of the Minor Arcana, as everything is relevant and holds a specific purpose. Everything has its meaning of importance in the grand network of the universe. Chaos and order are necessary components for creation and structure to the mystery of everything.

The Minor Arcana cards are the equally necessary variety of descriptive symbols, thoughts, emotions, states of being, non-action and action that purposely play linking roles in the assistance of integrating embodied wholeness.

All divine information is fractal narratives within narratives. All are connected. Some narratives are literal and obvious, while others are more complicated and require comprehension of apparent contradictions for the reader to absorb oxymorons that, on a deeper psychic and psychological level, make logical sense.

All cards will at least prompt the enquirer to investigate, and at best influence, deeper nuanced contemplation or trigger important and often necessary information to assist the reader. Either way, all information will be channelled, and or intuited, then translated accordingly, depending on the reader's capacity to absorb higher information, without concluding via conditioned veils of assumption. In other words, esoteric downloading of inner-realm information is always limited by an individual's association with words, as language and art only represent the unspoken truth that is held in all energetic fields. An awareness of what the message conveys is always the initiated magic art into the chaos field. Hidden coherent order is revealed when the seer sees. Where all dichotomies dance the dance of cosmic truth.

The *Mystical Realm Tarot* deck is intentionally straightforward in relaying information, both with illustrations and this booklet. I hand illustrated the images myself and chose a variety of historical eras, as I found this added interesting layers of visual content without misinterpreting the traditional meaning. I also decided to make some characters in the deck more inclusive so they were relatable to a diversity of readers.

This deck can be used to enquire about spiritual/psychological queries for an individual's journey in life. It can also simply be used to enquire about practical matters in everyday life and for love/romance enquiries.

Advanced tarot readers will be able to instantly use this deck without referral to the booklet. Beginner readers should have the booklet to assist them.

Like with any divination deck, sometimes the answers are plain and simple, other times the answers are convoluted, even contradictory. I feel the need to explain this because sometimes life is convoluted and contradictory. Sometimes two opposing energies can be uncomfortably together, simply because humans are complex and contradictory creatures! We need to learn the art of observing nuances and to not view life in basic black and white fixed terms. The more we are able to fluidly perceive life this way, the better we will be at reading double messages and all the grey areas in between of the human psyche. And the better we will be in reading tarot cards.

The *Mystical Realm Tarot* deck, like all divination decks, is a conduit of energetic information and energy shifts. So sometimes it pays to allow some time and revisit a specific question, because over time your energy and all energy is fluid and alters, either slightly or drastically. In other words, the divinations cards will pick up where you are at and your energy is never fixed.

I hope this deck will be another valuable deck to add to your collection. May you find it both inspiring and insightful, while also practical for everyday use.

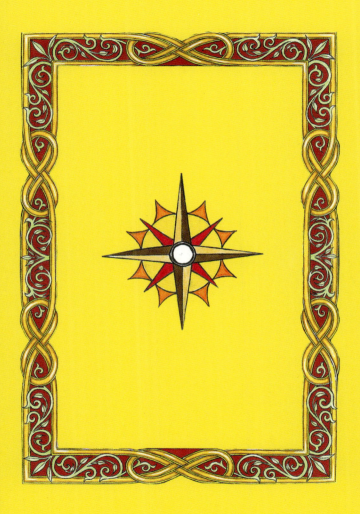

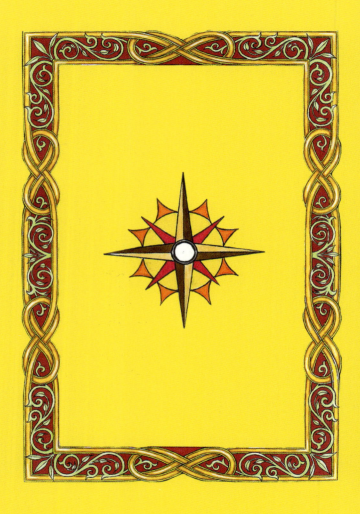

CARD
COMBINATIONS
EXPLAINED

Tarot cards are one of many divination modalities. Every card in a tarot deck is either a major or minor conduit representing a specific archetypal energy field.

All individual tarot cards, upright and reversed, have meanings that are fairly straightforward. However, sometimes the reader will experience a tarot spread that appears, on the surface, to be convoluted and contradictory.

This is because in the real world we experience external and internal contradictions, more than we'd like to recognise, with ourselves, others and the world in general. This is not necessarily a bad or good thing; this is just how reality unfolds sometimes depending on where we are at or where matters are energetically at at that specific time. Energy is always in flux and nothing is ever really fixed. Humans and reality are complex.

Life, thoughts, emotions, experiences, memories, beliefs, ideologies, personalities, values, culture, actions, habits and structures all add to the moving mix we call reality. Tarot cards will show you this too. Nuanced interpretation is required.

Reading tarot card combination spreads are no different. Sometimes the spread is straightforward and easy to read; other times card combination spreads require a still mind so the reader can intuitively read between the lines. Over time this becomes an art, simple to tap into energetically by channelling and downloading messages with ease. This is what the spiritual community labels as psychic ability.

Like any art, beginner tarot readers need to first learn the basic tools of what each individual card represents, then learn how card combinations can spell out. Sometimes certain tarot card combinations can shift and the perspective will alter regarding the relationships of card combinations. The number of card combinations that can be used are endless. This is why reading tarot cards is a high art, beyond just linear comprehension.

Below are some basic card combination examples to assist in perceiving beyond what appears at first glance a contradiction of coherent logic and reason. Logic and reason always expand to match the reader's level of consciousness. In other words, a narrow-minded person will have a narrow-minded set of logic and reason to rightfully back their insight and conclusion. Likewise, an expanded mindset of awareness will have an expanded mindset of logic and reason. All information is relative to the eyes reading it.

EXAMPLE 1

If you had the VIII Strength card next to the Ten of Swords card.

This combination is saying: even though a very painful ending or betrayal has happened (Ten of Swords), the person in question is holding out with grace, willpower, inner resilience and strength to plough through. Even though the individual's thoughts are causing them to hurt inside, for whatever reason, they are choosing to stay strong and persevere to the very end so things or matters do not fall apart.

EXAMPLE 2

If you had the XIII Death card next to the Ace of Cups card.

This combination is saying: a difficult shedding of some old way of being, thinking or doing is happening so room for a new way of being, thinking or doing can begin. The person is transitioning and evolving. The individual has done the inner shadow work and the higher self is integrating a higher level of self-love.

EXAMPLE 3

If you had the IV The Emperor card next to the Page of Pentacles card.

This combination is saying: the individual in question is being headstrong, structured, disciplined and a leader in their own right. Even though the individual is assertively standing within their own position of authority, they are choosing to give only a small token at present to show their sincerity.

EXAMPLE 4

If you had the VI The Lovers card next to the Five of Pentacles card.

This combination is saying: even though the individual in question is fully aligned with choosing love, they feel for the other, and this dominates their inner world. The person in question is simultaneously experiencing personal struggles that are influencing the individual's everyday life.

EXAMPLE 5

If you had the XVI The Tower card next to the Ten of Cups card.

This card combination is saying: a total shock and destruction of some description has occurred and affected the individual to the core. It has shaken the individual's sense of familiarity, comfortability and well-being. Something has shattered the individual; however, that individual is still hoping for some happy ever after.

Tarot spreads can vary in so many ways and always place each card into a relationship of dynamics according to the other cards in the spread.

The Major Arcana in a card spread will always place the major life lessons of energy coming through in an unfolding narrative. The Minor Arcana cards explain the Major Arcana's theme(s). If there are no Major Arcana cards in the spread, that means the story is still happening, and major life events have yet to manifest.

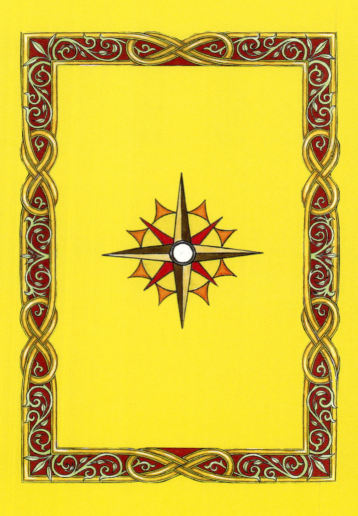

TAROT CARD SPREADS

THE 6W CARD SPREAD

The 6W card spread involves six specific questions pertaining to one overall themed spread. The 6W questions involve: who; what; when; where; why; and how.

The 6W card spread requires six cards – one card for each question.

The enquirer needs to have one specific theme to use the 6W card spread. The theme may be related to career, finances, love, family, friends and so on.

Before commencing the spread it is important for the enquirer to know their theme and write each question down on paper to ensure it relates properly to the theme.

I will give some examples here as to how to use the 6W spread.

EXAMPLE 1

6W SOULMATE/TWIN FLAME QUESTION SPREAD

CARD 1: Who is my soulmate/twin flame?
CARD 2: What do I need to know about them?
CARD 3: When will I meet them?
CARD 4: Where will I meet them?
CARD 5: Why are they my soulmate/twin flame?
CARD 6: How will I know it is them?

EXAMPLE 2

6W CAREER QUESTION SPREAD

CARD 1: Who can guide me in the right direction so I can achieve my dream career?
CARD 2: What do I need to know now for me to achieve my dream career?
CARD 3: When will I achieve my dream career?
CARD 4: Where will I achieve this?
CARD 5: Why am I having such trouble achieving this?
CARD 6: How well will I do in achieving this career goal?

EXAMPLE 3

6W BABY QUESTION SPREAD

CARD 1: Who will be the father of my children?

CARD 2: What will he look like?

CARD 3: When will I meet him?

CARD 4: Where will I be when I meet him?

CARD 5: Why have I not yet met him?

CARD 6: How will I know when I have met him?

Once the enquirer has written down all 6W questions they are to meditate while shuffling the tarot cards.

Once shuffled, place the six cards in order and the questions will be revealed within the cards. If the enquirer would like extra clarification, they can shuffle some more then place one extra card on top of every 6W card that is laid out.

Some readers prefer to use another oracle deck altogether as the clarifying cards. That, too, is an option as it can add a different layer onto the original spread. The original spread, however, is key to the questions.

PENTAGRAM SPREAD

This specific tarot spread is done by asking the question, 'What is blocking my ascension path?'

The spread involves placing five cards, after meditation and shuffling, into the pentagram star shape.

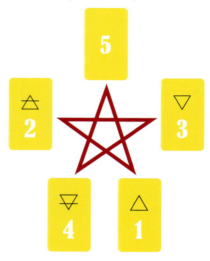

- The first card (card 5), the spiritual/ether card, is placed at the very top. This card represents the spiritual message for you at present.
- The second card (card 4), the earth element card, is placed at the far-left bottom corner. This card will represent the practical shadow message for you at present.

- The third card (card 3), the water element card, will be placed at the top right, slightly lower than the top first card. This card will represent the emotional shadow message for you at present.

- The fourth card (card 2), the air element card, is placed at the equal opposite side on the top left, slightly lower than the top card. This card will represent the mental/psychological shadow message for you at present.

- The fifth card (card 1), the fire element card, is placed on the far-right bottom, below the card above it and equally across from the far-left lower card.

The pentagram tarot spread is laid out in this order; however, the cards are read from last laid card to first.

- The first card read will be the fire (passions) card on the bottom far right.

- The second card read will be the air (thoughts) card on the top far left.

- The third card read will be the water (feelings) card on the top far right.

- The fourth card read will be the earth (practicalities) card on the bottom far left.

- The fifth and last card read will be the ether (spiritual) very top centre card.

Each card has a separate question regarding the enquirer's ascension shadow work questions. The questions each card represents are:

CARD 1: What passions of mine are blocking my path to ascension?

CARD 2: What thoughts of mine are blocking my path to ascension?

CARD 3: What feelings of mine are blocking my path to ascension?

CARD 4: What practicalities of mine are blocking my path to ascension?

CARD 5: What is Great Spirit trying to reveal to me now on my ascension path?

The pentagram spread is a shadow work spread and s showing us what we need to learn at this stage of our evolution regarding our personal ascension path. Like the previous spread, it is perfectly okay if people prefer to add one clarifying card to this spread for extra information. The original first card, however, is always the key point to ponder on at this stage. The clarifier is merely additional information to assist the first card's meaning and interpretation.

MAJOR ARCANA

0. THE FOOL

THE FOOL

The Fool is the very first card and represents the absolute beginning of The Fool's journey. It all starts at zero, the number before anything manifested. They are the infant, ready to take their first step into the unknown, totally untainted and unaware of what lies ahead.

The Fool is the most important card as all of everything, to everywhere, must firstly begin as The Fool.

The naive fool carries their small pack of luggage which represents their yet acquired baggage. The Fool at this stage carries no entrenched opinions or conditionings of their future path. The Fool has yet tapped into a phase of developed knowledge. Ironically, even though The Fool is inexperienced and ill-equipped, he is also exactly where he must be in order to take the journey of developing experience. For the zero must begin before matters come into being.

The mountains in The Fool's background are metaphors for the mounting obstacles and mysteries he must face, and hopefully overcome, in the future.

The small dog at his feet represents The Fool's subconscious's loyal dedication into the unknown. The Fool holds a small flower that is symbolic of his purity and innocence. The Fool is finally ready and prepared to embark on his path into awareness.

KEYWORDS

UPRIGHT
- Beginner's luck
- Inexperience
- Untapped potential
- The start
- Spontaneity
- New adventure

REVERSED
- Impulsive
- Lack of direction
- Stupidity
- Ignorance

I. THE MAGICIAN

The Magician, also known as The Maggi (Magus), is associated with the planet Mercury. He has one arm raised and one arm lowered and holds this stance to depict his activation of both spiritual and material manifestation.

The Magician knows he has entered into the embodiment of manifestation from the microcosm to the macrocosm. He holds his initiated position and access as a conduit of 'as above, so below'. He knows he must abide to the higher realms for the flow of energy into matter. He has positioned himself as the middleman agent, from higher realms down into the third-dimensional material realm.

The Magician confidently knows all are connected. He must always be humble in his awareness, for he also knows if he is not careful he can easily slip into a shadow shapeshifter archetype. The Magician must guard his charisma, insight and art, so he does not descend into a trickster through sleight of hand by hoodwinking his gullible fellow man.

He wears a purple velvet coat and top hat, which are symbolic of his natural connectedness and flow of the cosmic consciousness into his heart and head – the violet rays. His red tie symbolises his anchored base energies into the 3D material realm. His white blouse represents his purity and absolute respect of the magic arts.

He has with him the pentacle, sword, wand and cup. They represent his honourable relationship with the four elements: earth, air, fire and water.

The candle he holds is a metaphor for his illumination of the light within the dark. The ouroboros snake eating his tail belt is his reminder that he is eternally bound and self-contained in the regenerative and infinite cycle of life.

The infinity symbol above his head represents his connection and will into accessing the realms of eternity.

KEYWORDS

UPRIGHT
- Realised potential
- Manifestation
- Resourcefulness
- Willpower
- Action
- Opportunity
- Outwitting
- Success

REVERSED
- Manipulation
- Trickster
- Cunning
- Deception

II. THE HIGH PRIESTESS

The High Priestess is the archetype that represents the overseer into the unseen realms and all that is hidden from plain sight. The High Priestess is the gatekeeper for uninitiated meddlers ever entering into higher and forbidden realms.

She is the mediator of the realms and the keeper of wisdom. The High Priestess is the divine mistress, married to all that hides behind the veil of illusion. She is the oracle and the gateway into the unknown. The High Priestess is the embodiment of the sacred secrets, of the mystery schools and all esoteric teachings.

The High Priestess is the middle way, perfectly aligned inside the two great pillars which are associated with Solomon's hidden temple. The 'B' pillar Boaz is the pillar for strength. The 'J' pillar Jachin is the pillar for beginning. She is the master of bridging the two temple hemispheres into the central portal of pure consciousness. The two black and white pillars are symbolic of the dichotomy of division, the paradox of polarity and the secrets of duality.

The High Priestess is attached to nothing and connected to everything that is sacred and hidden. She gives nothing away. Her hidden knowledge is heavily guarded for she comprehends the futility of throwing pearls to swine.

The pomegranates hanging on the wall behind her represent fertility, abundance and her uncontaminated access into the feminine fruits of the underworld. Her blue habit represents the spiritual and psychic wisdom she embodies as a vessel for the great esoteric secrets. Her veil is symbolic of the mystical matrix of all non-physical realms and her divine marriage to all that is divinely hidden.

The sun and crescent moon above her head displays her crowning throne of enlightenment and illumination to all that is hidden. The High Priestess holds the Tora Scroll. This is showing how she holds in her hands access to all occult knowledge and the divine laws of the universe. The cross on her chest represents the divine intersection of time and space. The vertical line represents the ether, spirits, infinity, inter dimensions and cosmos, and the horizontal line represents the material, time and space. The red represents her courage, spirituality and psychic prowess.

KEYWORDS

UPRIGHT
- Divine feminine
- Sacred knowledge
- Insight
- Intuition
- Psychic
- Privacy
- Morality
- Receptive
- Wisdom

REVERSED
- Secrecy
- Confusion
- Disconnection to spirituality
- Mental blockage
- Emotional blockage
- Withdrawal
- Cognitive dissonance

III. THE EMPRESS

The Empress is beautiful and serene. She exudes relaxed confidence, unassumed power and gentleness. Her voluptuous, full-breasted feminine figure is early in pregnancy. The Empress embodies everything naturally maternal, lovable and nurturing.

As she comfortably sits on her luxurious throne of soft cushions she displays the delightful warmth and abundant nourishment she creates and gives to life. The Empress is showing she is the divine feminine, the soft comforting touch in this sometimes harsh world. Her simple pink dress represents pure love and her white under tunic represents purity.

She represents the abundant beauty, art, romance, love, sensuality, fertility and divinity of the creation of life.

She wears her empress headwear to show her position and divine archetypal title. Above her head shine 12 stars, displaying her sacred female position, synchronised with the cyclic years on earth. The 12 stars represent the 12 months of every cyclic year (the small star represents the non-full moon month in a natural cyclic year, of divine order of true time).

The Empress is the daughter of heaven and earth. She is the great earthly mother. She is Mother Nature, her natural cycles above and below, containing all her seductive, nourishing and sometimes terrifying seasons.

The flowing water behind her represents her organic and lucid connection to life, sustaining water and the oceans. Her pregnant womb is full of water and all life grows in or with water. Her fertile pregnancy represents her dominion over all growing life. Her sceptre has an orb on top, representing the female womb and divine feminine.

In the foreground is wheat, symbolising the crops of abundance, ripe and ready for the harvest.

She has a shield at her feet, with the feminine symbol of Venus. She is Venus. This represents the physical and energetic manifestation of real love.

The Empress is the personification of all the four Minor Arcana queen tarot cards wrapped in one.

KEYWORDS

UPRIGHT
- Pregnancy
- Beauty
- Nurture
- Maternal
- Art
- Love
- Abundance
- Productive

REVERSED
- Stagnation
- Unproductive
- Smothering
- Mother issues
- Fickle

IV. THE EMPEROR

The Emperor is the archetypal father figure. He is the stoic ruler of his realm and always gets the job done properly. He resides over his sovereign kingdom. He always leads and is a pioneer who initiates whatever is the wise path to obtain order, structure and success.

The Emperor sits on his throne adorned with rams' heads, which represent his personal relationship with astrological Aries and the planet Mars. Aries, the charging ram, being ruled by the head and Mars, the planet of war, both symbolise the psyche of The Emperor. (In Greek mythology the ram was used as a sacrifice to Zeus and holds similar archetypal forces.) The Emperor is also fiercely protective of his people and dominion.

In his right hand The Emperor holds a sceptre with an ankh at the head. This represents his hierarchical and ruling position over the key of life. The golden orb in his left hand is symbolic of earth, which he rules and oversees.

The Emperor wears red trousers, representative of his grounded power and passion in the material and ether realm. The red also symbolises his war-like fierceness to protect his people and kingdom from any intruding harm. His navy cloak is non-pretentious and symbolic of his authority, seriousness and disciplined rule of order.

At his feet he has a shield with a red eagle to represent his sense of protection and power over predators. His instinctive protective powers are where his divine masculine resides.

The Emperor would not win any charm competition, but he is always highly respected and deeply honoured by all in high positions. He is strict, strong, upright, straightforward, fearless, responsible and always takes accountability where need be. He is a true leader.

The Emperor is task-oriented, relentless and thorough. He respectfully knows what is necessary to bring sovereignty and wealth to his kingdom.

Above his no-nonsense face The Emperor wears his ram's-horn headwear to symbolise his virility and key warrior position in life.

KEYWORDS

UPRIGHT	REVERSED
◆ Authority	◆ Tyrant
◆ Stability	◆ Combative
◆ Initiative	◆ Violent
◆ Responsible	◆ Father issues
◆ Maturity	◆ Impatient
◆ Independent	
◆ Protective	
◆ Assertive	

V. THE HIEROPHANT

The Hierophant is sitting on his religious thrown inside a traditional place of holy worship. He is the male counterpart for the High Priestess.

On either side of him are two pillars. One pillar represents obedience, the other pillar represents disobedience.

The Hierophant's right hand points towards the heavens and higher knowledge while his left hand holds the triple papal cross. The three horizontal bars represent the Father, Son and Divine Great Spirit, as do the three crosses on his priest tie sash that sits over his spiritual robe. His mitre headwear displays his spiritual and religious authority. The golden crossed-key design on his headwear symbolises the keys of heaven he is entrusted to.

The two religious servants at his feet represent the passing down of sacred knowledge for institutions of spiritual order.

The Hierophant's red robe represents his position of spiritual authority regarding the esoteric mysteries of the cosmos, and the complexities of the human psyche.

The Hierophant stands for all that is traditional in values, and he also symbolically stands for the hierarchical institutions.

KEYWORDS

UPRIGHT

- Stability
- The Establishment
- Organised
- Patient
- Disciplined
- Traditional
- Conventional
- Mentor
- Marriage

REVERSED

- Unconventional
- Non-conformity
- Rebellion
- Questioning traditions
- Questioning authority

VI. THE LOVERS

The Lovers is all about relationships, close intimate connections and sincere heartfelt bonds between couples and partnerships.

The Lovers also pertains to having to face specific decisions of importance relating to a situation, complex decisions about lifestyle, sacrificial choices and all that is relevant to maintaining a sustainable, healthy commitment.

The nudity of the couple is symbolic of their mutual soul nakedness, which is honest and true to their mutual commitment.

The two trees in the background on either side are representative of the tree of divine knowledge and the tree of divine life. The serpent in the tree behind the female represents divine knowledge. The serpent holds the duality of both good and evil, wisdom and folly. The serpent is also a symbol of sensual temptation and the giver choosing this way or that, but all comes with natural spiritual consequences.

The tree with the DNA symbol behind the male represents the natural, physical and structural unfolding of genetic and biological codes passed down into third-dimensional evolutionary patterns for the lovers.

Angel Raphael, in between and above the lovers, represents the physical, emotional and spiritual healing forces blessed from the heavens that are available to the lover couple if they choose to connect to this gateway force.

The sun being grasped by Angel Raphael is symbolic of the joyful blessing open to them if they choose wisely.

KEYWORDS

UPRIGHT
- True love
- Twin flames
- Soulmates
- Wise choices
- Partnerships
- Mutual commitment
- Decisive
- Sincerity
- Blessings
- Romance

REVERSED
- Poor choices
- Indecisive
- Insincerity
- Break-ups
- Flaky
- Toxic relationship
- Non-committal

VII. THE CHARIOT

The Chariot displays a strong, brave warrior charging ahead with two Egyptian sphynxes driving his cart.

The warrior riding his chariot wears a golden suit of armour and a golden helmet. This represents his divine protection as he activates his golden will to move forth in balance with the universe. The five-pointed star symbol on his helmet is located in front of his third eye. This is to display his connection to not only forces above but forces below. He is attuned and has mastered the right action of the four earthly elements and the fifth heavenly portal element to generate momentum. The moon crescent symbols on both the warrior's shoulders represent his willingness to bear the weight of what is right, and the ability to move and charge ahead.

One sphynx is male, the other is female. This represents the masculine (electro) and feminine (magnetic) forces of duality generated throughout the universe. The two sphynxes also represent the two hemisphere forces within his own mind. One side being logic and reason and the other side being abstract and creative. He has wilfully mastered the necessary higher art of harnessing them both simultaneously and consciously by being in the middle. One sphynx is light and the other is dark. This too reveals the dual opposing forces that generate momentum of the universe outside and psychological universe within.

The Chariot is all about harnessing, via willpower, the positive and negative electromagnetic forces of nature that generate momentum and right action when wilfully aligned. The warrior is now willing and able to maintain control over his destination so long as he stays centred. He holds no physical reins for the two sphynxes and his conscious willpower is psychically and timelessly connected to the sphynxes' dual cosmic forces of generative power to charge forth.

The Chariot is also symbolic of the merkaba. The Chariot warrior has wilfully activated his light/spirit/body into conscious cosmic awakening. Nothing can hold him back now, as he owns the momentum to move ahead swiftly and can navigate and steer his path forward with confidence and determination.

KEYWORDS

UPRIGHT
- Willpower
- Activation
- Driven
- Motivated
- Momentum
- Action
- Movement forward
- Focus
- Goal oriented
- Self-control

REVERSED
- Stagnation
- Reckless
- No self-control
- Floundering
- No direction
- Aimless

VIII. STRENGTH

The Strength card shows an unassuming, quiet and serene woman gently touching an untamed lion. The lion responds with a yawn, expressing his total trust of the gentle yet powerful domination of the woman.

The once ferocious lion is now naturally softened and tamed by the woman's gentle caress. She teaches the wild animal that gentleness does not necessarily mean weakness. Through her softness, she reveals to the lion the powerful difference between base fight/flight/freeze reaction and relaxed, trusted, integrated power. The woman has, with no force whatsoever, energetically taught the wild lion how to choose a higher form of inner being and experience. The lion has integrated into a more evolved sense of presence purely through the woman's touch.

As she pats the lion's coat, she confidently and courageously reveals her vulnerable inner beauty to the lion; her warmth, kindness, comfort, affection and loving care.

The woman symbolises the powerful, courageous, strong and evolved aspects of care, kindness, compassion and empathy, all in conscious awareness. Her touch represents the transfer, energetically, of higher vibrational fields of awareness. These are connected to all, but need activation to trigger conscious receptivity to the sleeping, unaware animal within. She also represents the strength within to face what fears us, to overcome obstacles in our path, to achieve true success within. She is the powerful and compassionate path of least resistance. The woman is the symbol of the strength to overcome and conquer internal demons and destructive ego-scripted narratives within.

The woman also represents the courage to face fear and adversity for she knows she is connected to the infinite force of all.

Her simple, white, flowing tunic dress is symbolic of her innocence and purity of intention. The golden infinity symbol above her head represents her connection to eternal source. The flower band in her hair is symbolic of the connection to all that is simple, pure and beautiful, for within that hides great power, honour and pure strength.

KEYWORDS

UPRIGHT
- Honourable
- Strength
- Courage
- Strength of character
- Courage to be vulnerable
- Trust
- Influence
- Calmness
- Confidence
- Fearlessness
- Conquering self-doubt
- Self-control

REVERSED
- Distrust
- Fight/flight/freeze
- Cowardness
- Lack of self-control

IX

THE HERMIT

IX. THE HERMIT

The Hermit is an old bearded man, wearing an old hooded robe. He chooses to stand alone inside a cold, dark cavern. The Hermit holds a wooden staff in his left hand and a glowing lantern in his raised right hand.

The Hermit has self-imposed himself. He has chosen this in order to re-embark on solitary time, to self-reflect and ponder on who he is, where he is going and many more important questions.

His long grey beard symbolises his old age, mental maturity and acquired wisdom. The lantern he holds represents his inner world of enlightenment within the deep dark temple chambers of his mind. He is the internal explorer of hidden knowledge. He is the illuminated old one. The dark cave he stands alone in also physically represents the going within that is necessary.

The Hermit, in deep reflection mode, gazes hypnotically at small ripples within a puddle of water. As he gazes into his deep dark subconscious, new insights emerge from the dark unknown subconscious.

The Hermit knows he must revisit the dark abyss in his solitude to remember his gnosis within. He is at home with re-entering the dark mysteries and has done this many times. It is his ritualistic path to his own illumination and wisdom. He knows the descent down is the path to conscious ascension. He has already obtained high levels of spiritual knowledge and knows he has far more to insightfully know.

KEYWORDS

UPRIGHT

- Self-reflection
- Introspection
- Solitude
- Soul searching
- Isolation
- Wisdom
- Aloneness
- Gathering strength
- Pondering
- Deep first-person awareness

REVERSED

- Loneliness
- Fear of being alone
- Returning to society
- Constantly distracted
- Shallow
- Projecting
- Lack of any insight

WHEEL OF FORTUNE

X. WHEEL OF FORTUNE

The Wheel of Fortune card is all about the ever-changing cycles through the recurring passages of time.

The Wheel of Fortune image shows a giant universal wheel, with wheels within wheels in it, to symbolise the multilayered and multifaceted structure of the cyclic ways of the cosmos and all that spins, all within framework and by design.

Within the outer border of the wheel are the Hebrew letters YHVH, which mean divine source. This is to show that the divine creator has bound the cyclic moving pattern throughout time and space accordingly. Within this wheel is the word TORA, which means cosmic instruction and law. Rearranged, this spells ROTA, Latin for wheel. We also have TARO, the old word for tarot.

Within the wheel to the left is another cog wheel within a wheel moving through the passage of time. This represents human and earth passage of time.

The middle wheel contains the alchemical symbols for mercury, sulphur, water and salt. The outer corners contain the four elements to show earth's elements in space/time continuum.

Within the very centre wheel is the all-seeing observatory eye (I) of God, the conscious awareness, that travels consciously throughout all life within the wheel of fortune.

The four outer corners of the image are the four elements of earth to show the Wheel of Fortune is from the third-dimensional realm of perspective.

The Wheel of Fortune represents the cyclic passage of time and all of her recurring patterns and nuances within greater destiny. Things that occur to individuals in their own timeframe all play out often for seemingly mysterious reasons, but relevant and connected to larger wheels of fortune. Multifaceted and multilayered twists and turns in the Wheel of Fortune card can and do unravel themselves.

Both welcome and unwelcome change can come forth with the Wheel of Fortune card. However, sometimes a seemingly unwelcome change may be necessary for welcome growth. Vice versa, sometimes a seemingly welcome change may be necessary for unforeseeable hard lessons, for growth to occur. Good or bad, all movement to change is necessary in the game of life.

KEYWORDS

UPRIGHT

- Chance
- Good luck
- Cycles of time
- Destiny
- The time is right
- Fate
- Tide is changing for the better
- Good karma is coming

REVERSED

- Disappointment
- Bad luck
- Misfortune
- Unpleasant karmic lessons to learn
- Wrong timing
- Resistance to change

XI. JUSTICE

The sweet old, yet highly discriminating lady stands in between the two Solomon's Temple trees of balance. She delicately holds, in each hand, the equal sides of the scale of accuracy and true justice. Her silent and poised stance operates as the middle attunement for accurate assessment on matters.

The old lady of justice has integrated coherent logic and reason with sound intuition and instinct. She is the truth teller who holds intelligent, astute observation and nous with insightful sensitivity and care. As humble and harmless as she appears on the surface, she, in truth, is nobody's fool.

Around her throat chakra she has a triple-edged sword pointing to the earth. The sword represents truth, groundedness and unwavering finality in her decision. The triple-edged sword is also symbolic of the threefold karmic consequential outcome of action: what goes around comes around.

Her red dress symbolises her root chakra energies being anchored and solid. Her green cloak symbolises her open heart and integrity. Her elaborate red and green headwear holds the all-seeing eye. She is the all-seeing eye's ambassador.

The one white shoe, slightly peeking out from under her dress, represents that small quiet reminder that, sooner or later, everything chosen has natural consequences.

The square broach she wears on her cloak represents her crystallised clarity in discerning the truth. She sees through falsehood and truth and everything in between. Coercion, manipulation, bribery and soothsaying she does not participate in. She would die instead. She is justice and justice is truth. She cannot be hoodwinked.

She has no personal agendas in the outcomes. Fairness and justice are all she cares about. The lady of justice is unbiased, impartial and stands only for truth.

KEYWORDS

UPRIGHT
- Truth
- Integrity
- Equilibrium
- Fairness
- Justice
- Balance
- Legal matters
- Cause and effect
- Accountability

REVERSED
- Lies
- Imbalance
- Not taking accountability
- Corruption
- Injustice

XII. THE HANGED MAN

The Hanged Man is suspended from a tree. A snake, coiled up as a rope, is wrapped around his right ankle. The snake represents the wisdom The Hanged Man is acquiring during his sacrificial choice to be hung from a tree.

As he motionlessly hangs upside down, his reversed position begins his shift in perspectives on matters of life.

His unusual, reversed disposition appears to be a form of punishment. The reality, however, is that he has chosen to take this sacrifice to find himself more. Being hung in reverse is exactly what he knows he needs – to be still, not distracted and focused. He is suspended in space, poised and unwavering. The sacrifice is worth it to him.

The suspension in time has allowed him to pause in order to come back to himself. By turning everything upside down' his perspective has shifted, and he now has a new set of eyes to see with. The hanged man has let go of what he believed to be important and replaced this with a new, more mature level of awareness, uncontaminated with useless matters that he would once get caught up in. He is grasping reality on another level.

He wears old, stripy, patched up overalls without a shirt. This signifies his allowance to be plain, honest 'him', and not hang on to any pretence or false airs and graces. He has one large eye over his bare chest. This symbolises his new sight that he holds close to his heart. On his head he wears a hood, which only reveals some of his face, to show that he wants no distraction as he surrenders himself. The feather in his hood shows he knows this sacrifice will bring him good luck in the future.

The squirrel in the tree has collected some coins, which symbolises the eventual future blessings earned by him through letting go of all the nonsense he grasped on to and sacrificing himself to higher things.

The two sleeping bats, either side of him, represent letting go and developing new perspectives.

The ornate halo around his head reveals The Hanged Man has begun his initiation into illuminated consciousness through his sacrifice.

KEYWORDS

UPRIGHT
- Surrender
- Pause
- Letting go
- New perspectives
- Sacrifice
- Waiting
- Allowing
- New visions

REVERSED
- Avoiding sacrifice
- Resistance
- Stuck in old outdated patterns
- Delays
- Blocked vision
- Narrow-minded perspectives
- Shallow perceptions

XIII. DEATH

The Death card can be confronting, auspicious and feared by some. The Death card is, however, NOT about physical death. It is powerful and positive, for all new beginnings need an ending.

Death rides his white, magic horse of purity. Wearing his hooded royal blue robe, he holds in his right hand a black torn flag bearing the white five-petal rose. His flag symbolises beauty, purification and immortality within the cycle of life. The five-petal rose also symbolises profound metamorphosis.

He, Death, is the living skeleton that metaphorically represents the framework that lives on after skin is shed away. The three openings in his skull are beautifully decorated to honour magic, creation and transformation. He carries with him a scythe that represents endings and harvest for new creation of life.

The two towers in the background represent the gateway Death has passed through to enter into the magic cycle of profound transformation.

The Death card is all about graciously surrendering and letting go of what no longer serves us in order for new life to be activated and born into us.

KEYWORDS

UPRIGHT

- Endings
- Transformation
- Profound change
- Metamorphosis
- Moving forward
- Releasing attachments
- Graciously surrendering

REVERSED

- Resistance to change
- Delayed endings
- Long-term illness
- Depression
- Unfulfilment
- Clinging to what no longer serves you

XIV. TEMPERANCE

The Temperance card is depicted by the angel delicately pouring the living, flowing waters of life back and forth between two vessels in an artful motion. This represents the magic flow of the two opposing cosmic forces of active masculine energy and receptive feminine energy. These polar opposite forces are the divine inner/outer, inhale/exhale, yin/yang energies of life. The balanced send/receive water motion from one vessel to the other is the sacred alchemy the angel is incapsulating. The yin/yang symbols on the copper vessels represent this.

The winged angel is in harmony with the flow of life. She is one with the source, at peace and in control of her unfolding sacred flow. She perceives deeply the divine value of the balancing dance of duality and is in alignment with cosmic receptive and active forces.

The Temperance angel wears a soft blue flowing dress, which externally reflects her internal calmness and watery flow with natural energies. She does not force. She delicately dances with the forces and slips into a divine path within that flows without.

Around her neck she wears a red triangle within a yellow square broach. The triangle represents the triple embodiment of the body/mind/soul aspect of the human temple. The square around the triangle represents the earth, and all her natural laws of the material realm.

She delicately dips her bare right toes in the gentle flowing waters. This represents her gentle connection to the natural ebbs and flows and rhythms of sacred higher conscious life. Simultaneously, she has her bare left foot standing on the ground, which represents her anchored connection also with the natural laws of the material and physical realm. Both energies travel through the soles of her feet. This represents her soul absorbing everything. She is the embodiment of artfully blending complex dualities into divine harmony.

On her forehead she displays the circled dot symbol. The dot represents her I-AM-ness being activated within her temple. The yellow iris flowers represent the wisdom she embodied through the alchemy of merging opposing forces of the cosmos.

KEYWORDS

UPRIGHT
- Going with the flow
- Alchemy
- Balance
- Harmony
- Moderation
- Internal calmness
- Peace
- Composed
- Restraint

REVERSED
- Imbalance
- Excessive
- Impatient
- Internal battle
- Reactive
- Addicted to drama
- Triggered off balance

THE DEVIL

XV. THE DEVIL

The Devil is depicted as the horned goat of Mendes or Baphomet – half goat, half man. He stands on his hooves on top of his boxed-in pedestal. He screams with dominance, pleasure and pain within his indulgent realm of complete darkness and ignorance of anything sacred.

The Devil is the ruler of his animalistic kingdom. He is bound in his kingdom. All three figures are bound in this realm.

Below him are a naked woman and man with chains around their necks. They are at the complete mercy of their master. This woman and man have small horns and animal tails. This represents their absence of higher consciousness and addiction to base animal pleasures – totally disconnected from higher awareness. The man and woman stare at their god in awe and bewilderment, which shows their learned helplessness and inability to unbind from their prison of addictive pleasure.

The Devil has total dominion over his realm, which offers endless pleasures, addictions and all excesses that bind. The Devil appears powerless to exit the pleasures that bind him and his slaves appear powerless to unchain themselves from The Devil.

The Devil has enormous bat wings, which shows he metaphorically sucks the creative life blood out of his victims of prey. He is a demigod ruler of the flesh. On his chest he has an inverted red pentagram. This symbolises he is owned only by third-dimensional materialism and pleasures and has no concern or comprehension of anything divine. All is fair game in his bounded kingdom. Higher frequencies of consciousness are forbidden in his realm. The Devil is totally divorced from his higher self, as are his captured prisoners.

The Devil's kingdom cares solely about hedonistic pleasure, for that is all he and his worshippers can energetically embody.

KEYWORDS

UPRIGHT
- Excessive self-indulgence
- Sexual lust
- Physical pleasure
- Temptations
- Materialism
- Addictions
- Oppression
- Powerless
- Psychological imprisonment
- Learned helplessness

REVERSED
- Releasing addictions
- Detachment
- Freedom
- Developing higher awareness
- Reclaiming personal power

XVI. THE TOWER

The Tower on top of a rocky island has been struck by lightning. The natural disaster has shattered the entire structure. Smoke and fire engulf and consume everything inside The Tower.

The Tower represents the psyche of the individual. The lightning hitting The Tower represents forces that are out of the individual's control and have shattered their preconceived concepts of what was. These forces are sharp, sudden, shocking and difficult to process and accept immediately.

The fire and smoke in The Tower represent a total spiritual cleansing.

The complete destruction and obliteration of The Tower head is symbolic of the individual's psyche being completely shocked, possibly even traumatised at whatever has unfolded into their awareness. Everything that was, in a blink of an eye, no longer is.

This also symbolises the opening and activation of the crown chakra, shattering all previous delusions, forcing cosmic higher consciousness into being.

The rising rough waters below The Tower represent the emotional body starting to feel unpleasant feelings that he/she would rather not feel.

The two small, flimsy trees flanked either side of the crashing tower represent the individual's psychological and spiritual reference polar points, which are now being forced to face something materially, conceptually and emotionally challenging.

The universal forces have intervened by destroying what was, in order to cleanse and totally rebuild something stronger, wiser and better.

KEYWORDS

UPRIGHT
- Danger
- Crisis
- Shock
- Collapse
- Destruction
- Chaos
- Sudden revelation
- Sudden unexpected change

REVERSED
- Trauma
- Loss
- Volatile situation
- Resisting change
- Denial of cold hard facts
- Delaying the inevitable

XVII. THE STAR

The Star card shows a naked young lady sitting near flowing water, with one foot placed in the water.

She sits alone in the beautiful night holding a water jug in each hand. She pours water from the jug in her right hand back into the great flowing waters. This symbolises the vast subconscious realms within her and also in cosmos. She also pours water from the jug in her left hand so water pours onto the dry land for nourishment. This symbolises aspects of her subconscious becoming aware and growing into consciousness, all designed within the cyclic pattern of the evolutionary growth of all life, spiritually and physically.

She perceives with sublime serenity and gratitude the splendour and magic of fractal universe, both inside and out.

Her nakedness is symbolic of her transparency and vulnerability. She knows her vulnerability when she is renewed is where her divine power rests. She trusts in the divinity of all things true. She trusts herself.

The tree in the background symbolises the tree of life and the secret nutrients of divine life. The white bird represents peace of mind and divine thought.

The night sky is dominated by one enormous star, which is symbolic of her spiritual essence and her higher ascended self. The other seven, smaller stars represent the seven chakras that need to be healed for wholeness. They also represent the seven sisters linked to the Pleiades. The bright stars in the dark night she sits under also represent her inner state, where she can navigate in the dark within, for her healed energies are beacons of light consciousness sparkling the path to see through the veil of illusion.

KEYWORDS

UPRIGHT
- Inspiration
- Renewed hope
- Spirituality
- Faith
- Self-trust
- Rejuvenation
- Positivity
- Serenity
- Peace of mind
- Opportunity

REVERSED
- Despair
- All hope lost
- Negativity
- Lack of faith
- Despondent
- Missed opportunity
- Trust issues

XVIII. THE MOON

The Moon dominates this tarot card. Her great full-phase face is asleep in the quiet night sky. She is dreaming within the matrix. The Moon gives off her soft, dim, reflected light from the distant sun. She is at home in the dark. Her light only reflects in the hidden dark.

The Moon dreams and travels into the unknown.

Beneath and in front of The Moon stands a domestic dog and a wild wolf, facing each other, howling up to The Moon's mysterious frequencies. The dog represents the civilised and higher nature of humanity. The wolf represents the feral and lower nature of humanity.

The two towers in the distant background represent the opposing dualities residing in all human psyches. One aspect of the mind destroys (evil) while the other aspect of the mind creates (good). Both towers have winding, descending paths that lead to the dog and wolf. This symbolises the winding paths of subconscious.

The Moon symbolises the ambiguous, multi-perspective confusion and complexities in truly deciphering good from bad.

In the very centre of the foreground lies a crayfish, crawling out of its safe and familiar pond. This represents the infancy stages of consciousness emerging from humanity's primordial ignorance.

The Moon is the great reflector. She is the mysterious mirror that magnifies and projects back to us all that we are at within our own subconscious ignorance and emerging conscious states of being.

KEYWORDS

UPRIGHT
- Illusions
- The matrix
- Intuition
- Subconsciousness/ unconsciousness
- The mystery
- Anxiety
- Secrets
- Unclear
- Confusion
- Deception
- Dreamy states
- Perplexed

REVERSED
- Insomnia
- Mysteries unveiled
- Coherent clarity
- Release of anxiety
- Weird dreams

XIX. THE SUN

The Sun tarot card is very easy to read, obvious and is simply the most positive trump card in the entire deck.

The brilliant, blazing, bright sun smiles contently and honestly over all life he shines upon. He is the bringer of life and symbolises overall optimism that he generates into life.

He is the glory and the great shining one. Metaphorically, The Sun is the light at the end of a dark tunnel. He brings honesty and blessings to life. The Sun is satisfied and represents everything good and enlightened. He is everything beautiful that makes your heart sing with joy and bliss.

Under the vibrant sun is a playful, spirited, innocent child standing on top of his magical white unicorn. The child represents the true happiness that is generated from the pure and innocent, carefree inner child within all. The child symbolises the natural euphoria we feel when we are in tune with our authentic true self.

The white unicorn is representational of the purity and magic our spirits manifest and embody when we are open for joy to enter into us.

The sunflowers replicate The Sun. Smile and dance for The Sun, for it is the source of life on earth.

The Sun is uncomplicated. He is what he is. He is the blessing moments of bliss.

KEYWORDS

UPRIGHT
- Happiness
- Joy
- Euphoria
- Contentment
- Vitality
- Success
- Confidence
- Optimism
- Honesty
- Enlightenment
- Openness
- Unconditional

REVERSED
- Unhappiness
- Pessimism
- Closed off
- Misery
- Conceited
- Sadness
- Conditional

XX. JUDGEMENT

The Judgement card has Archangel Gabriel (the strength of God) flying through the sky to deliver divine source messages.

As Angel Gabriel soars through from the heavenly realms she blows her golden trumpet to call for attention to humanity with awakening eyes that see and ears that hear. Attached to her trumpet waves a golden flag bearing the symbol of the red ankh. This represents the key to eternal life.

Beneath Angel Gabriel is a half dead, grey, mummified man, woman and child. They arise from their ancient Egyptian decorated sarcophaguses. This is metaphorical for the resurrection, the rebirth, the phoenix rising, the restoration from being asleep to life's lessons into being reborn back into awakening.

They stand with outstretched arms up towards Archangel Gabriel, awakening from the big sleep. This symbolises humanity's opportunities to read the signs placed forth from the universe, to awaken from the hazy social conditionings most sleepers fall into.

This card is all about self-assessment of our beliefs, insights, decisions, why this is so and what will we learn from this.

KEYWORDS

UPRIGHT
- Sound judgement
- Redemption
- Analysis
- Absolution
- Recovery
- Inner calling
- Self-evaluation
- Purpose
- Awakening
- Constructive criticism
- Call for attention
- Learnable

REVERSED
- Poor judgement
- Self-doubt
- Self-criticism
- Condemning
- Unteachable
- Punishing

XXI. THE WORLD

The World tarot card is dominated by a naked cosmic woman swirling in the great universe. She cyclically swirls inside the great universal ouroboros snake.

She holds two golden batons, one in each hand, symbolic of the willpower and energy required to complete any cycle. She circles the world within her. She has a massive red ribbon swaying and swirling around her rotating body. This symbolises her successful completion of a major cycle.

The World represents the evolutionary, completed motions of perceived cycles relevant to the world's standpoint. She also represents the evolutionary completed motions of perceived cycles relevant to the heavenly realm's standpoint. The World card is about the necessary space to breathe and float before the next major cycle begins.

The woman in the World tarot is suspended in the heavenly realms, encompassing her beloved world. The cosmic ouroboros snake, eating its tail, encompasses her. This represents the eternal cycles of life that must be completed.

Outside of the ouroboros, in the heavens, are four character images, one at every corner: the woman, the eagle, the bull and the lion. They are representational of the four fixed stellar navigational signs of the solar system – Scorpio, Aquarius, Taurus and Leo. They also represent the four elements of our world – water, air, earth and fire.

The World card holds many layers and is also about expanded perspectives of our outer world, the ability to go back into our inner world and the completion of all the cycles we achieve within the cosmic pattern of the universe.

KEYWORDS

UPRIGHT
- Completion
- Integration
- Accomplishment
- Travel
- Wholeness
- Achievement
- Possibilities and probabilities
- Perspective
- Hindsight
- Foresight
- Executed goals

REVERSED
- Seeking shortcuts
- Cheating
- Delays
- Emptiness
- No goals in life

MINOR ARCANA

ACE OF PENTACLES

ACE OF PENTACLES

A massive golden pentacle coin sits inside a huge nest on a large branch of a solid tree. The branch is shaped like a cupped hand, cradling the nest with the large pentacle coin.

This one large pentacle represents an obvious and new material and/or financial opportunity that is presenting itself.

The solid tree the nested pentacle is on symbolises that the opportunity is grounded, practical and securely planted in 3D reality. It is not some pie in the sky dream or sham scheme. This may be regarding a new business, new job/career, a new stable and secure relationship. Whatever it is, it is a sensible and profitable investment all round.

The branch resembling a giant cupped hand is revealing that the offer being shown is stable, grounded, reliable and is not going away.

The surroundings show a golden winding path that travels from the anchored-in tree footings to the far mountainous horizons. The golden path travels through a lush green hedge with an archway. The path represents the reliable way available. The lush, arched hedge the path travels through represents prosperous doorways open to those who stay on the right path. The mountains in the far distance represent life's obstacles, which are inevitable but surmountable if we sensibly stay ambitious and on the right path.

The white lily flowers at the foot of the tree symbolise prosperity guaranteed if we are fully committed to staying the course.

KEYWORDS

UPRIGHT

- New financial career opportunities
- Available resources
- Stable offer
- Ambitious
- Good investment
- Reliable partnerships
- Prosperous
- Egg-nest security
- Substantial money saved
- Realised potential
- New home
- Sensible money sense
- Financial manifestation

REVERSED

- Lost opportunity
- Lack of planning
- No foresight
- Scarcity
- Sham
- Scam
- Flimsy
- Fickle
- Bad investment

TWO OF PENTACLES

TWO OF PENTACLES

The Two of Pentacles shows a fit and flexible young man in a joker costume. He is juggling two pentacle coins while simultaneously balancing on a piece of board on top of a blow-up ball.

His joker outfit is symbolic of his ability to not allow life's problems to take him down. It is divided into two colours, which represent opposing obstacles and tasks that need to be fulfilled. The red line in the middle is representative of the fine line of focus and balance in between that is necessary to manage all tasks.

The two juggling pentacles are inside the infinity symbol. This signifies he can handle managing unlimited problems and tasks that are often universes apart in skill level.

The Two of Pentacles male is displaying his flexibility in multitasking by both juggling the two pentacles and balancing on a wobbly piece of board on a ball. He has mastered the fine art of managing many opposing tasks simultaneously. The Two of Pentacles is resourceful and can handle all the rough and rocky patches life throws at him with adaptability, efficiency and ease.

He is symbolic of someone who knows what to place energy into and what to release. He is agile and a swift decision maker when it comes to prioritising what is needed and what is not and balancing all that is required simultaneously with grace and aptitude.

Behind him is the ocean with crashing choppy waves. This water is symbolic of all the emotional and practical problems life throws at us.

The two ships rocking and swaying are symbolic of the human capacity to become flexible and adaptable, to graciously ride the unsmooth and disruptive ups and downs of life. The two ships are also representational of the human vessel's resilience and ability to not sink and drown in life's challenges.

KEYWORDS

UPRIGHT
- Time management
- Prioritising
- Adaptable
- Flexible
- Multitasking
- Multiskilled
- Capable
- Aptitude
- Resourceful
- Quick thinking
- Self-management
- All-rounder
- Efficient

REVERSED
- Overcommitted
- Disorganised
- Inefficient
- Chaos
- Overwhelmed
- Inept
- Overextending
- Amateur
- Drowning in life's problems

THREE OF PENTACLES

The Three of Pentacles shows three artists collaboratively working together on a wall mural in a church at night.

The artist on the far left appears to be the leader of the team; he is studying designer plans. The other two artists on the right are in the process of painting pre-designed angels on the wall.

Being night and having lit candles around reveal this team have a deadline to complete the contracted project. The scene also reveals the utmost dedication the three workers are fully committed to.

It is clear these three specialists are highly skilled and competent in their field of expertise and are capable and expected to deliver the planned project on time. They are working harmoniously, seriously and cohesively as a group, with each individual participating in accomplishing the necessary planned goals. They are all on the same page and have no interest in swaying from this.

In the rear wall of the church there is a large circular window containing the three pentacles, symbolic of what this image represents.

The Three of Pentacles is all about the union and coming together of skilled people aiming to produce and deliver and collectively aiming for the one goal.

KEYWORDS

UPRIGHT

- Teamwork
- Collaboration
- Learning
- Implementation
- Pooling energy
- Shared goals
- Deadline accomplished
- Co-operation
- Alliance
- Joint effort
- Association
- Work partnerships
- Union

REVERSED

- Working alone
- Not being a team player
- Conflict of interest
- Resisting groups
- Division
- Non-co-operation

FOUR OF PENTACLES

The Four of Pentacles shows a defensive, haughty man pompously clinging to his four pentacle coins: two pentacles held under his arms, one pentacle above his head and one pentacle under his feet.

The Four of Pentacles snobbishly holds his head high in the air, with his self-ordained crown of importance on his head. He proudly exhibits his high-end clothing of exotic cloth.

What he represents is obvious: he is a materialist, concerned only with being stingy in his hoarding and desperately attaching himself to whatever he believes will serve his self-interest at whatever cost. He has lost his sense of humanity.

A rat next to him, simulating his pose, is symbolic of his inner self-centred world that cares for nothing besides what his greedy hands can materially get a hold of. He finds himself alone on the cobblestoned streets of his village, showing his total disconnection to all that was human in himself. His jaded, uncaring side has fully adopted his material, possessive and selfish nature.

He has become a total prisoner of his own greed.

KEYWORDS

UPRIGHT

- Clinging on
- Greed
- Savings
- Frugal
- Control
- Stingy
- Taking
- Closed off
- Selfish
- Possessive
- Distrusting

REVERSED

- Generosity
- Giving
- Openness
- Overspending
- Selfless
- Trusting
- Letting go

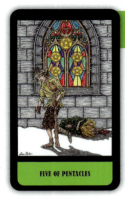

FIVE OF PENTACLES

The Five of Pentacles portrays a desperate and despairing image where we witness two impoverished, starving, homeless people struggling outside a lavish cathedral. They are freezing cold in the snow.

The man is bandaged, seriously wounded, and hobbling around with a makeshift crutch. The woman lies freezing and huddled on the cold snow up next to the cathedral outer wall.

Both are in filthy torn rags and totally unkept. They are visibly outcasts, rejected and abandoned from respectable society.

The reality for the two people is beyond bleak. All hope has abandoned them.

The cathedral behind them displays solid grey brick walls that separate them from the other side. Dominating the cathedral brick wall is a massive, exquisitely designed stained glass window with vibrant colours being reflected from the warm lighting inside. This shows that the inner state of the two individuals' psychological and spiritual support system has abandoned them in their dire time of need.

KEYWORDS

UPRIGHT

- Financial loss
- Abandonment
- Lost hope
- Despair
- Unemployment
- Disgrace
- Shame
- Scandal
- Homelessness
- Outcast
- Extreme struggle
- Bankruptcy
- Adversity
- Loneliness
- Spiritual poverty
- Material poverty

REVERSED

- Recovery from financial loss
- Overcoming adversity
- Redemption
- Feeling welcomed
- Forgiveness
- Positive change
- Hope returning

SIX OF PENTACLES

The Six of Pentacles shows a very well-dressed man of status and wealth handing out gold coins to two bedraggled beggars who are on their knees.

He wears a plush fur coat, and in his left hand holds a golden set of balancing scales for his golden coins. This is representational, not only of his literal, material bank balance, but also is metaphorical of the energy bank balance within himself. That is, he has his own inner tank full of flowing energy and therefore has plenty of quality and substance, energetically, to give back to those who are empty and in need.

The Six of Pentacles image is symbolic of authentic, unconditional generosity that has no hidden agenda. The wealthy man represents not only material generosity, but also spiritual, psychological and emotional generosity.

This card is all about the act of giving and receiving and how this aspect of humanity is vital for individuals, communities and societies at large. For without such generosity, a society is doomed to moral decline, evolutionarily speaking.

KEYWORDS

UPRIGHT
- Giving
- Generosity
- Charitable
- Sharing
- Assistance
- Supportive
- Unconditional
- Donations
- Community
- Society

REVERSED
- Exploitative
- Unpaid debts
- Pity
- Disgust
- Martyrdom
- Conditional
- Superiority complex

SEVEN OF PENTACLES

The Seven of Pentacles shows a farmer attending to his crops with a hoe. He has done most of the hard work already and gently checks his crop's developmental stages in growth. The Seven of Pentacles knows all good things come into fruition slowly and timely. He understands metaphorically and literally that a good harvest requires not only specified effort and hard work but also perseverance and patience to allow the correct timing of executing a quality harvest.

The Seven of Pentacles is a hard-working farmer who paces himself to nurture what is required to achieve long-term goals.

He wears his trusty old patched up, worn out but strong overalls. This is representational of his inner world where he too is also trusty, patched up and fatigued but strong. He is resilient and has what it takes to follow through in all seasons of life, to do what is needed to get the job done. He has foresight and he knows everything has a time and a season and everything must be tended to at the correct time if long-term goals are to be achieved.

KEYWORDS

UPRIGHT
- Sustainable outcomes
- Perseverance
- Investment
- Long-term goals
- Foresight
- Vision
- Growth
- Results oriented
- Appreciation

REVERSED
- No long-term goals
- Waste
- Impatience
- Lack of vision
- Lack of foresight
- No appreciation
- Unfinished work

EIGHT OF PENTACLES

EIGHT OF PENTACLES

The Eight of Pentacles shows an old man carefully labouring at mastering his etching of his pentacle. He is surrounded by all his necessary tools for his developed craft. This represents that he has developed the inner tools and functioning he needs to achieve what he is skilled in.

He wears his trusted old work apron as he works on his craft, which is symbolic of the hard-earned repetitive training and apprenticeship that has earned him the self-mastery he has developed in his specialised skillset.

In his workshop he has eight pentacles displayed, which shows he has developed a high standard of sought-after skills. He has developed high-quality techniques and is valued and in demand.

The Eight of Pentacles is the quiet achiever. He is never easily distracted from his craft. He has perfected his attention to detail into mastery. His expertise sells itself, for he has mastered the grade through earned training and proficient skill.

Outside of his rustic workspace it is cold and snowing. This reveals he is focused, resilient and accomplishes nothing but the best, even when conditions and external factors are against him.

KEYWORDS

UPRIGHT

- Apprenticeship
- Repetitive tasks
- Developed skills
- Mastery
- Motivated
- Dedicated
- Hard-working
- Attention to detail
- Self-employed

REVERSED

- Laziness
- Dead-end job
- Sloppy
- Easily distracted
- Misdirected

NINE OF PENTACLES

The Nine of Pentacles shows a poised, well-dressed woman of refinement sitting peacefully in her garden of plenty.

She sits with her pet falcon resting on her gloved left hand as she gazes beyond her gated garden. The falcon represents her astute intelligence, intellectual prowess, disciplined self-control and self-generated power. The falcon also represents she is the overseer of all her enterprising endeavours.

She is the personification of embodied self-agency and self-made independence. The garden she sits in is representational of the harvested fruits of her own labour.

The yellow dress and headwear she is attired in are symbolic of her sophisticated capacity to use her intellectual strength and mental aptitude to acquire financial independence. The basket of fruit sitting at her feet is symbolic of her self-made prosperity.

She stares beyond her guarded gates, which are decorated with nine pentacles. This displays her long-term visions that she protects with healthy and solid boundaries.

The Nine of Pentacles is resourceful, skilful and disciplined. She knows her self-worth and is highly protective of who she is and what she stands for. She is unapologetic about her self-directed and self-generated ambitiousness.

The Nine of Pentacles is self-made, self-disciplined and autonomous.

KEYWORDS

UPRIGHT

- Luxury
- Self-sufficient
- Autonomy
- Leisure
- Self-made
- Skilful
- Accomplished
- Social status
- Self-reliant

REVERSED

- Hustling
- Living beyond your means
- Reckless
- Arrogant
- Superficial

TEN OF PENTACLES

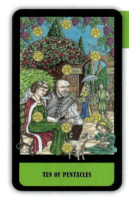

TEN OF PENTACLES

The Ten of Pentacles card is dominated by an ageing husband and wife. They are content and comfortably relaxing in the family gardens. The loving couple watch over their granddaughter, who is joyfully playing with the family dogs. The dogs represent the loyalty the family are bonded into.

The old couple are respectful, eloquent, traditional, educated, mature and refined. This reveals the decency and honour they have earned through intelligence, hard work and honesty.

In the background are the old couple's daughter and son-in-law chatting. They symbolise the ongoing respectability and sensibility passed down for generations to come.

The family gather and relax in their shielded gardens, full of lush fruits, which represents the solid safety and protection of all the abundance they have successfully achieved and inherited.

The refined wealth and security the traditional family display goes beyond material wealth. This family embodies spiritual, psychological and emotional blessings of value in abundance. The family has deep-rooted class and values all that is good and decent.

The entire scene is all about comfort, reliable security, sophistication and abundant prosperity.

UPRIGHT

- Respected
- Financial security
- Roots
- Family security
- Comfort
- Affluence
- Solid foundations
- Old money
- Ancestry
- Traditional
- Trust funds
- Family home

REVERSED

- Disrespect
- Disinheritance
- Financial loss
- Debt
- Unsophisticated
- Family disputes
- Breaking traditions

PAGE OF PENTACLES

The Page of Pentacles depicts a young male holding a pentacle. This represents his sincere and humble offering. He stands diligently in a field with an abundant spectacle of small wildflowers. The blooming wildflowers symbolise the Page of Pentacles' abundant goals, which he has mentally planned out and psychologically manifested.

The young Page of Pentacles stands tentatively looking over a fence that is symbolic of his protective nature towards the goals he has chosen to manifest. Behind the fence are freshly ploughed fields and distant lush trees. This is symbolic of his solid promise of complete sincerity to slowly achieve the positive outcome he has planned.

The Page of Pentacles is fully aware of what is in front of him. He will fulfil his promise. He is not reckless and even though his offering is humble, he knows this is the first stage necessary in working towards what he wants to achieve.

The youthful Page of Pentacles wears earthy green and brown attire, which represents the grounded, practical and earthy ways that comprehend materially what is required to achieve his goals.

He wears a contrasting bright red hat with a feather in it. This is representational of the private drive, determination and hope that his promise will become a reality.

Outwardly he is low key, methodical and consistent. Internally he is driven and sincere.

KEYWORDS

UPRIGHT
- Progress
- Consistent
- Becoming
- Sincere promise
- Small token
- Loyalty
- Pledge
- Earnest
- Oath
- Paced
- Opportunity
- Achiever

REVERSED
- Procrastination
- Lack of progress
- Inconsistent
- Missed opportunity
- Underachiever
- Insincere promise

KNIGHT OF PENTACLES

The Knight of Pentacles stands stoic and stationary next to his reliable black horse. He is dressed in full armour and holds his helmet in his right arm. He raises his pentacle, cradled in his left hand. This all reveals he offers himself as the predictable, prepared man you can rely on, no matter how long a task takes. He is fully present, committed, honest and steadfast. He knows what he must do.

In the background lie endless fields of organised crops. This represents the Knight of Pentacles' patient, slow-moving and persistent methodology to get all the tasks done properly. He is in no hurry and no corners are cut to complete his long-term goal.

The Knight of Pentacles is slow, thorough and routine. He is never rushed or sloppy and will slowly tick all the necessary boxes off one by one.

The Knight of Pentacles is focused, cautious and careful. He does not do anything by half measures. He is the one you can 100 per cent rely on.

KEYWORDS

UPRIGHT

- Slow moving
- Conservative
- Safe
- Reliable
- Routine
- Patient
- Diligent
- Predictable
- Thorough
- Careful
- Cautious
- Stoic

REVERSED

- Perfectionism
- Impatient
- No initiative
- Fickle
- Workaholic
- Reckless
- Sloppy

QUEEN OF PENTACLES

QUEEN OF PENTACLES

The Queen of Pentacles sits on her golden throne gently holding her golden pentacle, which reveals the prosperity she acquired with her own hands.

The Queen of Pentacles wears a simple green dress with a light floral shawl around her shoulders. She quietly and contentedly sits with bare feet. This symbolises she is connected to Mother Nature and is authentic, modest and unaffected by material prosperity.

She stares off into the distance with a slight look of contemplative care and concern, which shows her sincerity, natural thoughtfulness, responsibility and kind-hearted ways.

The Queen of Pentacles is surrounded by lush, flowering plants and trees symbolic of the abundance and security she has earned through diligence and hard work.

Around her feet are two white rabbits. They represent her fertility and consistent energy.

The Queen of Pentacles is refined, yet earthy and natural, organised and a sweet, nurturing mother.

KEYWORDS

UPRIGHT

- Nurturing
- Hard-working
- Dependable
- Sensible
- Gentle
- Kind
- Practical
- Prosperous
- Generous
- Organised
- Sincere
- Refined

REVERSED

- Greedy
- Gold digger
- Selfish
- Materialistic
- Home wrecker
- Disorganised
- Insincere
- Unrefined

KING OF PENTACLES

KING OF PENTACLES

The King of Pentacles is ambitious. He sits on his golden throne, legs folded, holding his golden sceptre in his right hand and a pentacle in his left. This displays he is down to earth, practical and unassuming in his ways, while also being an excellent businessman.

His golden throne has two golden bulls carved on each side, which symbolises his earthy, grounded nature that provides and protects.

The King of Pentacles wears a simple brown coat with fur, and is shirtless underneath. This reveals his unpretentious practicality and willingness to do the hard work and get the job done at any time.

Near him, he has his reliable dog, which is no thoroughbred, but is loyal to the end and hard-working. The king is trustworthy and all the servants of his kingdom are loyal to him.

Surrounding the King of Pentacles are plentiful grapevines that symbolise the abundance he has acquired through effort and discipline.

In the far distance is his castle, which shows what he has acquired through sensible leadership and discipline.

The King of Pentacles is quietly intelligent, efficient, enterprising and highly responsible.

KEYWORDS

UPRIGHT
- Discipline
- Business
- Prosperous
- Leadership
- Security
- Stable
- Sensible
- Reliable
- Provider
- Hard-working
- Responsible
- Loyal

REVERSED
- Financially inept
- Stubborn
- Unreliable
- Gambler
- Lazy
- Irresponsible
- Status seeking
- Senseless

ACE OF CUPS

ACE OF CUPS

The Ace of Cups is depicted with a hand holding a massive golden grail rising out of the depths of the great ocean.

This golden grail has five waterfalls streaming out of the full chalice. The five streams of flowing water represent the five senses that are fully in tune, awake and flowing from the individual soul's illuminated cup within.

The two golden entwined snakes, coiled in a heart-shaped embrace, represent the individual's heart, body, mind, chakra and soul's open integration and wholeness that is overflowing with self-love and has much more to share.

The white dove above the chalice carrying a golden host represents the individual's ascended consciousness and elevated feelings of internal peace and radiant love that overflows from their heart and soul.

The golden host held by the white dove symbolises an individual's psychological, emotional and physical embodiment of true love from within.

At the core of the Ace of Cups is pure, abundant and overflowing adoration and sweet true love.

KEYWORDS

UPRIGHT

- Self-healing love
- New romantic love
- Newfound excitement
- Bliss
- Abundant creativity
- Open heart chakra
- Spiritual awakening
- Agape love
- Amora love
- Rebirth
- Overflowing inspiration
- Renewed love of life
- Emotional/spiritual fulfilment
- Totally inspired

REVERSED

- Emptiness
- Emotional loss of love
- Self-loathing
- Blocked creativity
- Uninspired
- Lacking love of life
- Going through the motions in life
- Unloved
- Feeling loveless
- Closed heart chakra

TWO OF CUPS

TWO OF CUPS

The Two of Cups shows a young couple embracing and tenderly kissing as they salute their golden cups.

The couple are publicly pledging their sincere and mutual love and desire for each other as they ceremoniously raise their golden cups of engagement together for all to see.

The Two of Cups is all about shared true and dedicated love, mutual respect and romance equally exchanged between two souls.

Behind the kissing couple is the giant lion-headed, winged caduceus of Hermes Trismegistus, his Mercurian staff with the two snakes coiled around it.

The winged lion's head represents the fiery chemistry and sexual passion the couple are mutually and energetically surrounded by for each other.

The giant winged lion also represents the chimera that knows all transactions are powerful and need to be treated with caution, care and respect to avoid passion turning into vitriol.

The two snakes entwined around the wand represent a mutual energy exchange, intelligent negotiations and compatible enterprising trades.

The loving couple know wholeheartedly the seriousness of commitment and respect, for they also know the blessing of commitment if they sincerely honour and respect each other above all else. They understand sexual passion alone is not enough grounds to sustain a true relationship. Love, honour, open communication and utmost respect for each other must rule.

KEYWORDS

UPRIGHT
- True love
- Mutual respect
- Unified commitment
- Flourishing partnerships
- Soulmates
- Compatible
- Engagements
- Proposals
- Marriage
- Sexual passion
- Open, honest communication
- Win/win
- Wise negotiations
- Mutual trust
- Mutual faithfulness

REVERSED
- Break-ups
- Separations
- Divorce
- Closed/concealed communication
- Tension
- Division
- Kiss of death
- Win/lose
- Foolish negotiations
- Incompatible
- Distrust
- Cheating

THREE OF CUPS

THREE OF CUPS

In the Three of Cups we see three beautiful, young and happy adults smiling, celebrating and dancing in a circle together.

The two young ladies and one young male all raise and salute their golden cups of champagne to bless and express their positive gratitude that they are celebrating together. Everyone is ecstatic and full of absolute bliss and joy.

All three friends are clearly very happy, appreciative and delighted to be united and are embracing the good times.

The blonde female and male appear to be brother and sister. The brunette appears to be the male's counterpart and sister-in-law to the blonde.

It is autumn. Golden leaves naturally fall around the three happy dancing souls like confetti. This is symbolic of the timely shedding of all past things that no longer serve them.

The large, golden ripe pumpkins growing in front of the three friends represent timely prosperity, blessings and dreams coming true, all ripe, ready and on time for harvest for all involved.

The two ladies have bouquets of yellow flowers to symbolise their happiness. One holds her bouquet of flowers, showing she has found love and blessings. The other female tosses her bouquet of flowers in the air, representing her found love and blessings also, which she sends and shares with others who wish and hope for the same. The male is happily and gratefully connected to the two females. All three are excited to share and unite their blissful abundance.

FOUR OF CUPS

FOUR OF CUPS

In the Four of Cups we see a despondent and forlorn peasant woman sitting alone under a tree on top of a green hill.

She stares aimlessly into space completely oblivious of the three golden cups standing in front of her. The woman is more concerned with her self-engrossed pessimism of life.

She is also totally unaware of the cloud to her right offering her a golden cup with a red heart etched into it. She is beyond even caring for new offers of love. She is way too broken inside, jaded and tired. Boredom, apathy and indifference to everything is all she feels. Reality is nothing but a banal duty and endlessly unrewarding chore for her. Her passion and zest for life have completely abandoned her. She sits alone on top of the hill wondering where her hope has gone. Her heart is no longer in anything.

Beside her sits her basket containing two loaves of bread. This represents a sustainable soul of abundance and nourishment is within her, yet she is unwilling to notice. She is more self-absorbed in her depression. She has lost trust and hope for anything outside of her no matter how positive it appears.

The three golden cups in front of her, which she completely ignores, represent her apathy in trying. She cannot summon the will to even see positivity in front of her. She is merely existing in her dark nights of the soul. She does what she must but is dead inside.

The small mouse next to the three cups represents accomplishments that she has made yet is unable to see, for all she sees is veiled by her internal darkness.

The sleeping owl, tucked away inside the tree, symbolises that her wisdom and strategy for life are presently asleep as she drags her disillusioned self through her depression.

Her indifferent, jaded soul can see no hope in anything anymore and is blindly ignorant to what is possible and right in front of her.

KEYWORDS

UPRIGHT

- Apathy
- Forlorn
- Depressed
- Indifference
- Bored
- Unimpressed
- Melancholy
- Weariness
- Stagnation
- Lost hope
- Downhearted
- Dispirited
- Jaded
- Lost faith in humanity
- Feeling dead inside
- Dread

REVERSED

- Retreating
- Choosing happiness
- Clarity
- Awareness
- Resuming hope
- Seeing light at the end of the tunnel
- Regaining zest for life
- Regained faith in humanity

FIVE OF CUPS

FIVE OF CUPS

The Five of Cups shows a slouched, cloaked man with his head held down as he sits alone and weeps tears of sadness.

His tears are red, like blood, which is symbolic of the raw and heartfelt pain he is feeling and expressing.

Next to him are three visible cups that have fallen over with red wine spilling out onto the earth. This is representational of the heartache and emotional loss that is pouring out from him.

The fact that he is only aware of these three lying down cups reveals that his thoughts and emotions are only focused at present with his pain and despair.

The man in mourning is completely unaware or unprepared or unwilling to focus on the two upright cups behind him. He is not ready to face the positive opportunities and potentials that are right near him.

The riverbank he sits on overlooking the running river is symbolic of his running emotions.

The bridge in the far distant background is representative of the opportunities he will need to face by building a bridge and getting over it. He, however, is not ready to be positive and hopeful in doing this. His sorrow has taken centre stage in his psyche. The fact the bridge is in the far distance also reveals in the future he will be able to see this.

KEYWORDS

UPRIGHT

- Grief
- Loss
- Regret
- Guilt
- Sadness
- Disappointment
- Failure
- Mourning
- Heartbreak
- Emotional baggage
- Emotionally hurting
- Loneliness
- Feelings of hopelessness

REVERSED

- Self-forgiveness
- Moving on
- Self-healing
- Seeing positives
- Regained hope
- Contentment
- Acceptance

SIX OF CUPS

SIX OF CUPS

The Six of Cups shows two young children playing gleefully in a rural homestead garden. The little girl swings happily on a swing under a large blossoming tree. The little boy is tenderly offering the little girl a large golden cup filled with pink roses. The pink roses are symbolic of sweetness and innocent, unconditional love.

Surrounding the little girl and boy are plants all in bloom with a range of colourful flowers. This is representational of youthfulness and unconditional love.

In the background is a family cottage signifying comfort and safety.

In the foreground are five more golden cups containing a variety of bunched flowers, which reinforces the all-round unconditional love and affection that is felt and in bloom.

The entire scene represents sentimental memories of a time that was simple, lovely, innocent and uncomplicated.

The two small children are fully present and are not bound up in past or future concerns. There are no hidden agendas and what you see is what you get. Life is untainted and harmonious. They are safe and secure and in full innocence with love for life and each other.

KEYWORDS

UPRIGHT

- Childhood memories
- Sweetness
- Nostalgia
- Revisiting the past
- Sharing
- Reminiscing
- Familiarity
- Tender feelings
- Yearning
- Unconditional
- Sentimentality
- Homesick

REVERSED

- Stuck in the past
- Lacking playfulness
- Too serious
- Childhood issues
- Childhood abuse
- Immaturity
- Conditional
- Cynical

SEVEN OF CUPS

SEVEN OF CUPS

The Seven of Cups shows a young female comfortably lying on her stomach playing with a pearl necklace as she daydreams and contemplates a diverse range of desirable and undesirable fantasies.

Each golden cup represents seven inventions of her imagination.

The golden cup with a handsome man in it represents romantic idealism. The golden cup with a pink- and red-striped castle represents her fanciful desires for material security and comfort. The masked lady represents her own masquerading in life. The snake in the golden cup represents her fears and wisdoms. The wreath in the red-bowed golden cup represents her desire for winning, fame and accolade. The treasure chest with golden jewellery represents her desire for wealth, beauty and nobility. The ferocious dragon represents the deep-rooted fears she dreads to face.

All of these dreams she has are not innately bad in any way whatsoever, for all great outcomes initially need a dream. Dreaming does hold a place to fertilise the passion a soul needs to initiate a path suited to them, the best of anything manifested and actualised needed to start as a dream.

The Seven of Cups, however, does caution against the danger of constantly wasted time in dreaming the best and worst in this and that, without ever physically and mentally doing the hard work to achieve or overcome what is in the head. It is sensible to speculate about everything but living in a fantasy land is a wasted life.

The Seven of Cups suggests you be very careful what you wish for, for everything is never fully what it appears. All choices have benefits, but do not be fully fooled by the allure.

KEYWORDS

UPRIGHT

- Self-delusion
- Lots of options
- Lost in fantasy
- Daydreaming
- Indecisiveness
- Illusion
- Procrastination
- Building castles in the sky
- Unrealistic
- Speculation
- Multiple possibilities
- Sleepwalking through life
- Easily distracted
- Daring to dream big

REVERSED

- Total confusion
- Overwhelmed by choices
- Complete disarray
- Awakening from wishful thinking
- Becoming grounded
- Down to earth sensibility
- Being realistic

EIGHT OF CUPS

In the Eight of Cups we see a red-robed woman holding a stick for support as she quietly walks away from something. She is walking alongside a calm water's edge while a full moon lights the night sky.

This card is all about walking away. As sombre as she is, the woman understands this is the right choice.

The Eight of Cups woman is clothed in a long hooded coat dragging along the wet shore. This is symbolic of her maturity and deep-rooted passion for all she knows is right and good. As painful as it is, she must follow her heart's truth for what she knows is right and good for her. She has no ill will but must do what she must do.

The night scene is symbolic of her deeply searching within to truly analyse the situation. Her choice may appear regretful; however, she understands whatever she must let go of is for her higher good. This is no knee-jerk reaction.

The decision to walk away hurts her heart deeply – the eight dented and seriously damaged cups show this clearly – but to stay would hurt her even more.

The full moon is symbolic of the realisation she has entered a type of death only to be rebirthed.

KEYWORDS

UPRIGHT
- Disappointment
- Walking away
- Letting go
- Soul searching for the truth
- Looking deeper
- Seeing the truth
- Self-analysis
- Quiet acceptance
- Fatigued
- Weariness
- Decisiveness
- Emotional strength
- Loneliness

REVERSED
- Aimless
- Drifting
- Indecisive
- Fear of change
- Lost
- Staying in a bad situation
- Avoiding facing the truth
- Seeking revenge

NINE OF CUPS

NINE OF CUPS

The Nine of Cups depicts a well-rounded man sitting contentedly in his abode. He comfortably sits on an expensive Persian rug on the floor with one large golden cup resting on his foot. Near him is a bowl of fresh fruit.

The Persian rug is symbolic of the worldly attributes he has acquired through intelligence and hard work. The bowl of fresh fruit in front of him is symbolic of the fruits he has earned through his own efforts.

The Nine of Cups is attired in lavish yet elegant Middle Eastern headwear and clothing. He is unashamedly adorned with expensive and fine jewellery. This represents the abundance he has acquired himself.

The Nine of Cups is totally at ease and comfortable with where he is at and what he has achieved. He chooses to openly sit on the floor to show his natural ease with being around all levels of society. He knows and respects in his heart all hierarchical diverse platforms that know how to work hard, like himself. He is wealthy but not a snob.

Behind him are two white-tableclothed tables. Both tables have four golden cups. This is symbolic of his satisfaction and contentment with what he has spiritually and materialistically achieved, both internally and externally. The white tablecloths are symbolic of his open heartedness and purity at heart. The dual table setting in the background also represents celebrations, gatherings and parties.

The Nine of Cups has earned everything he has. He is rightfully highly pleased with himself and totally grateful for all he has acquired.

KEYWORDS

UPRIGHT
- Emotional fulfilment
- Satisfied
- Grateful
- Rewards earned
- Acclaim
- Wishes come true
- Contentment
- Fame
- Popularity
- Celebrity
- Self-confidence
- Happiness
- Celebrations

REVERSED
- Smug
- Delusions of grandeur
- Snobbery
- Ungrateful
- Notoriety
- Arrogance
- Greed
- Unhappiness

TEN OF CUPS

TEN OF CUPS

The Ten of Cups shows a happy family playing outside their lovely cottage home in their lovely flowering garden.

The mother and father stand romantically and lovingly arm in arm, both with one arm openly raised up towards the arched rainbow. The rainbow, with 10 golden cups above, is representational of the abundant blessings they have finally achieved after previous sorrow and hardship. This family stuck it out united as a loving family through thick and thin. Now they are reaping the golden rewards for enduring and staying 100 per cent committed.

Just in front of the embraced parents are their three lovely young daughters frolicking, giggling, laughing and dancing happily.

They, as a family, are fully content and exceptionally happy with their blessings and bliss. They know they earned it honestly and deserve everything beautiful they have. This family has endured heavy loads in the past and now they reap the rewards of their previous devotion to family, determination to persevere and commitment to stay united. They love life and their treasured friends and most of all their wonderful and precious family.

The green hills in the background are symbolic of their fertility.

The sun shining inside the arched rainbow of golden cups is symbolic of divine blessings, happiness and joy.

KEYWORDS

UPRIGHT
- Blissful relationship
- Total contentment
- Happy home
- Earned blessings
- Fulfilment
- Domestic harmony
- Security
- Family blessings
- Long-term relationships
- Happy ever after
- Children
- Stable relationship
- Play
- Fun
- Family reunions and gatherings

REVERSED
- Misaligned values
- Struggling relationship
- Disconnection
- Domestic conflict
- Isolation
- Separation

PAGE OF CUPS

PAGE OF CUPS

The Page of Cups depicts a youthful male flamboyantly dressed in bright colours. He wears a navy blue floral tunic with hot pink tights and under top, matching headwear with a big flowing green feather and a light green flowing shawl. This represents an idealistic person who is young at heart and naive still to the complexities of life.

In his right hand he holds a golden cup that has a green fish jumping out. This is displaying the Page of Cups' fanciful sense of wonder. The fish jumping out of the cup is also representational of his dreamy take on life that is still mostly preoccupied with fairy tales and the magic wow factor of life.

The Page of Cups is fully in touch with his inner child, which helps him maintain a high level of innocence and creativity. He is stylish but not yet a man. He still is far more interested in fluffy fantasy.

The Page of Cups prefers the glamour and allure of the frivolous aspects of life. He is still mesmerised by how things appear on the surface and has not yet developed a mature and less-lavish take on life.

He may appear somewhat shallow but he is not a bad person. He is naturally intuitive but has not grown up fully yet.

The ocean behind him reflects the Page of Cups' flowing creativity and his intuitive side. The clouds in the air are representational of his head being in the clouds.

KEYWORDS

UPRIGHT

- Curiosity
- Possibilities
- Hunches
- Dreamer
- Frivolous
- Crush
- Stylish
- Fashion
- Youthful
- Idealism
- Innocence
- Living in fantasy land

REVERSED

- Creative block
- Doubting intuition
- Escapism
- Neglecting inner child
- Emotionally vulnerable
- Show off
- Uses shock factor for attention

KNIGHT OF CUPS

KNIGHT OF CUPS

The Knight of Cups gently rides on his golden horse. He is holding up a golden cup with two red roses, looking towards the person he is charmingly gesturing his offer to. This symbolises his heartfelt and peaceful message of romance and hoped for acceptance of possible love.

The Knight of Cups wears his metal armour suit, which represents that he is ready and armoured, psychologically prepared to receive at worst a rejection, and at best acceptance from his offer. If he is rejected he will accept it graciously. He is very attracted to the person in question and is prepared to put himself romantically out there.

The horse is walking at a gentle pace and is adorned in red attire. This is reflective of the Knight of Cups' gentle calmness and earnestness. The red on his horse and armour represents his desire and romantic feelings.

The wings on the Knight of Cups' helmet are representational of his creative imagination.

The flowing river behind him is symbolic of his flowing feelings and how he desires to openly share this with his person of interest. He wishes and hopes for reciprocated feelings.

The Knight of Cups is chivalrous, tactful, peaceful and romantic at heart.

KEYWORDS

UPRIGHT

- Romance
- Idealist
- Chivalry
- Gentlemanly behaviour
- Attraction
- Romantic gesture
- Dating
- Tactful
- Imaginative

REVERSED

- Jealous
- Tactless
- Over-imaginative
- Moody
- Vanity
- Disappointment
- Tantrums
- Avoiding conflict

QUEEN OF CUPS

The Queen of Cups is depicted by a beautiful, serene and gentle lady who is dreamily sitting on her soft pink throne by the edge of the ocean.

The Queen of Cups holds in her right hand a large and ornate golden cup that is sealed with a lid, which represents her capacity to quietly and elegantly contain yet feel all the deep feelings that emerge from the depths of her subconscious and soul.

Her long flowing dress and headwear are a soft blue. Her flowing shawl is a soft pink. These depict her naturally gentle and soft ways.

Her feet are tucked under her gown and are kept dry and away from the water's edge. This shows that the Queen of Cups has mastered the art of maintaining a poised and po.ite position in public so as to not be overwhelmed and engulfed by demonstrative emotions from deep within her. Her feelings and emotions are private and not for anyone in the world to witness. She is selective about whom she openly reveals her tender and loving soul to.

The Queen of Cups is connected and in tune with the flow she feels very deeply within. However, her reserved nature always maintains public emotional poise and stability.

She is more shy than demonstrative and is the sweetest, most sensitive soul ever, who feels love deeply for herself and for others.

The seashells surrounding her represent her femininity and serenity and her divine connection to unconscious realms.

KEYWORDS

UPRIGHT
- Emotional stability
- Romantic feelings
- Sentimental
- Compassionate
- Imaginative
- Intuitive
- Healer
- Private
- Dreamy
- Supportive
- Shy
- Beauty

REVERSED
- Co-dependent
- Needy
- Clingy
- Fragile
- Insecure
- Emotionally unstable

KING OF CUPS

KING OF CUPS

The King of Cups depicts the king seated on his elaborate throne of gold, positioned stably and securely while being surrounded by the great waters. This represents he has total control and balance over his emotions and thoughts.

His throne has two golden dolphins either side that symbolise his equally balanced emotions and intellect.

The King of Cups displays a soft, caring and gentle face. This shows he is not afraid to reveal his more sensitive side. He embraces his vulnerable nature without ever losing sight of who he is. The King of Cups is very connected to who he is and therefore connects equally well with others, which is his key to perceiving nuanced subtleties in others. As open hearted as he is, his high sense of rationale and reason always stay with him on his endeavours.

The King of Cups is calm, approachable, sensitive and diplomatic. Even though he can wear his heart on his sleeve, he also holds earned wisdom and sincerity. He is gentle natured, but never erratic or foolish. He holds an open cup of wine, symbolic of his devotion and love.

He is a romantic at heart who is captivated by true beauty, creativity and loveliness. However, what he feels he does not flaunt. The King of Cups is devoted to all people, places and things that he holds dear to his heart.

The King of Cups is compassionate and caring. He listens to all. He is empathetic and kind. He is mature in his perceptions and has mastered emotional intelligence.

His sweet nature can sometimes be confused as naivety. Naive he is not: his head and heart are finely tuned in.

The King of Cups is highly intuitive and perceives on another level. His kind, easy-going nature and well-mannered demeanour have earned him much love and few enemies.

KEYWORDS

UPRIGHT
- Diplomatic
- Balanced head and heart
- Devoted
- Wise
- Sensitive
- Compassionate
- Romantic feelings
- Affectionate
- Mature
- Easy-going nature
- Gentle
- Well-mannered
- Emotional intelligence
- Sympathetic
- Open hearted

REVERSED
- Undevoted
- Naive
- Cold hearted
- Manipulative
- Repressed
- Insensitive
- Crude
- Heartless

ACE OF WANDS

ACE OF WANDS

In the Ace of Wands we see a giant hand holding a giant sprouting wand coming out of a raging fire of flames.

The entire image is symbolic of renewed, newfound energy all fired up and fully activated. The fire represents passionate energy and drive.

The sprouting wand indicates the new ideas and opportunities that are being born and growing as well as real potential and expansion.

The Ace of Wands is always positive news bringing in fresh beginnings that are sparked with excitement. Passion, vitality and highly energised forces are always with the Ace of Wands.

The Ace of Wands is forever ignited in a positive way and fully ready to take the challenge on.

The background of the image shows a horizon that has been burnt to ashes. The ash-ridden landscape reveals a psychological and spiritual cleansing that was needed in order for renewed life to be reborn.

The castle in the far distance is symbolic of a promise of new opportunities soon to arrive and be birthed into existence from all that occurred previously.

The sun and rays from the sun behind the wand represent the new passions coming into being.

The Ace of Wands is bold and daring and ready to follow the passions that are now ignited in them.

KEYWORDS

UPRIGHT

- Inspiration
- Spontaneity
- Potential
- Creative spark
- Vitality
- Enthusiasm
- New opportunities
- Excitement
- New initiative
- Urgency
- Getting in the game
- Getting fired up
- New lease on life

REVERSED

- Lack of inspiration
- Delays
- Loss of enthusiasm
- Passionless
- Creative blockages
- Lethargic
- Hesitancy

TWO OF WANDS

TWO OF WANDS

The Two of Wands depicts an Egyptian leader who stands on his balcony in between two large wands, overlooking his community. He holds in his left hand a small globe of the world.

The two large wands bolted on his balcony represent the two important choices he must decide between. The fact that the two wands are on his balcony and he is in the middle of them indicates he has yet to fully make his decision and needs quiet time to think within his comfort zone.

In front of him, in the community he presumably rules are two dirt roads that take two distinctly opposite directions and end at polar opposite destinations. This symbolises the choices he must make. Each path has opposing gains and opposing losses. He knows the grass is never greener on the other side and all decisions have natural consequences. He also knows that he needs to decide, for stagnation is not good for him.

The man gazes motionlessly into the small globe he holds as he mindfully transcends into an inner state of coherence and clarity of being to assist his decision making. The small globe is more than a point to gaze into; it also represents the sheer size, magnitude, potential possibilities and weight of this decision, whichever way he chooses. He knows what could be at stake and does not take this decision lightly.

He overlooks two distant sailing ships far off in the distant Nile River, which symbolises what can be gained either way in his decision making.

He knows he cannot procrastinate on his decision. His right hand behind his back, with fingers crossed, indicates his hope that he makes the correct decision.

KEYWORDS

UPRIGHT
- Crucial moment
- Future planning
- Insightful inquiry
- Progress
- The first step ahead
- Calculated risk taking
- Anticipation
- Critical thinking
- Realistic
- Pivotal
- Analysing
- Unbiased processing
- Decisive
- Potential possibilities
- Coherence
- Weighing up pros and cons

REVERSED
- Unrealistic
- Jumping the gun
- Wishy-washy
- Indecisive
- Dithering
- Procrastination
- Stuck in a rut
- Ambiguous

THREE OF WANDS

THREE OF WANDS

The Three of Wands shows a finely dressed woman standing alone high up on a barren sand dune in the desert, watching her camel train of cargo in the distance slowly arrive more closely to her.

She stoically stands on a hill holding at arm's length one of the three wands firmly placed into the ground high above for the cargo train to find its destination.

In the foreground behind the woman is a fine Turkish rug laid out with quality refreshments for the journey workers who have delivered her ship of treasures, which is symbolic of her delayed gratification as she has patiently waited.

The image tells a long-awaited story that indicates the goods have travelled a long, arduous journey to finally arrive at their true destination. The image is representational of the individual's long journey to eventually taste the feelings of success through lengthy overseeing, planning, organisation and above all visionary foresight and skill.

The woman in the image is the overseer of the entire project. She looks ahead and waits for what she has previously set in place. She understands at the core, the meaning of delayed gratification in order to succeed.

She stands alone. She is a self-made autonomous woman who creates her own path in life. This card is all about the individual who has harnessed intelligent decisions in order to reap the rewards.

She dared to broaden her horizons and see what was really out there for her in this world, then pursue and obtain this with her own skill and ability.

Her self-agency has finally brought her goods in.

KEYWORDS

UPRIGHT
- Progress
- Expansion
- Foresight
- Overseas opportunities
- Forward planning
- Entrepreneur
- Growth
- Delayed gratification
- Playing big
- Global trade
- Self-agency
- Autonomy
- Broad-minded

REVERSED
- Playing small
- Unexpected delays
- Restrictions
- Limitations
- Obstacles in the way
- Narrow-minded
- Lack of progress
- Sell-out
- Instant gratification

FOUR OF WANDS

FOUR OF WANDS

The Four of Wands shows a lovely bridal couple blissfully inside four cornered wands posted together by a canopy of blossoming wreaths.

The yellow bouquet tossed away by the bride represents the happiness they share with each other and the happiness they give to others.

Each connecting wand displays a red ribbon tied in a bow. These four red ribbons represent the stable, reliable, romantic intimacy that is mutually loyal from both the bride and groom.

The happy groom, carrying his equally happy bride, represents an equally binding sexual union between two consenting adults. They desire the public's awareness that their mutually grounded, solid commitment is real.

The four large standing wands represent the couple's mutually satisfying union, which they have announced and are celebrating to the public. The four wands also represent the reliable and dependable foundation of stability both are committed in sharing to support each other in life.

The entire celebratory image symbolises a celebration of the mutual obligation, mutual stability, mutual belonging and mutually reliable roots both have finally accepted to be true and of authentic value.

The beautiful fenced off manor in the background with the pebbled path that leads to the couple in the canopy represents and reinforces the security and harmonious belonging to successful prosperity the couple have now entered into.

KEYWORDS

UPRIGHT
- Celebration
- Mutual trust
- Joyful commitment
- Blissful connection
- Belonging
- Weddings
- Security
- Happy reunions
- Laying down roots
- Harmonious home
- Intimate bonding
- Romantic connection
- Welcoming surprises

REVERSED
- Lack of roots
- Unwelcome surprises
- Falling into separation
- Home conflict
- Not belonging
- Transient
- Instability
- Sexual scandal

FIVE OF WANDS

The Five of Wands depicts a chaotic, aggressive scene with five angry people holding their wands in the air as weapons, seemingly against each other.

Four people with wands in the background are divided into two sides attacking each other. Clearly this aspect of the scene indicates there is a division or clash of ego regarding some point of contention.

This, however, only reveals half of the story. The fifth man, a prominent leader, shows an angry man waving his wand like a weapon towards people we do not see in the image at all, while the group in the background continue to squabble among themselves.

This leader adds an invisible twist to the assumed scene. This very man adds the possibility that the real enemy is not even visible and all of this could very well be an in-house, political division. The more we observe this image, the clearer it unfolds that in-house conflicts of interest are unfolding even though all involved are representational of the very same tribe.

Either way, tension has built and the division is rippling out.

The leading character is, however, fully aware where the true source of division is coming from.

KEYWORDS

UPRIGHT

- Politics
- Tribalism
- Extremism
- Conflicts of interest
- Disagreements
- Arguments
- In-house division
- Chaos
- Rivalry
- Clash of egos
- Diversity
- Tension

REVERSED

- End of conflict
- Agreements
- Peace
- Truce
- Tensions released
- Co-operation
- Treaties
- Unity
- Diplomatic negotiations

SIX OF WANDS

SIX OF WANDS

The Six of Wands depicts a man standing on his horse and holding up his wand in relief. His wand has a victory wreath attached to it.

Around the victorious man is a crowd holding five wands in support of and praise for the man's successful achievements.

The five men around the Six of Wands man are symbolic of the public and transparent recognition the man rightfully earned. Interestingly, one wand is held by a person we cannot see, which symbolises some private support and praise from a specific source that is not yet revealed.

The Six of Wands has earned his stripes and is victorious. He completed all the goals required to win in the end.

Everything about this card symbolises the individual in question has attained public victory. He/she has successfully achieved, with flying colours, the outcome that was necessary after enduring hardships and fulfilling their required endeavours.

The Six of Wands has gained rightful public accomplishment due to their commitment to hard work, focus, discipline, willpower, strategy and personal nous.

Through all that was thrown at them they never gave up and therefore have come out the other side victorious.

KEYWORDS

UPRIGHT

- Victory
- Success
- Recognition
- Self-confidence
- Win
- Triumph
- Praise
- Acclaim
- Supporters
- Fame
- Celebrity
- Rewards
- Being in the spotlight

REVERSED

- Fall from grace
- Failure
- Lack of recognition
- Lack of achievement
- Disgraced
- Shamed
- Loss of confidence

SEVEN OF WANDS

SEVEN OF WANDS

The Seven of Wands depicts a man on top of a rocky hill armed with one large wand as his defence weapon against six battling opponent wands beneath him.

The Seven of Wands is well positioned to defend his territory. Even though he has six wands attacking him, the Seven of Wands has the higher ground to defend himself.

He represents the struggles we must face in order to achieve rightfully earned success. The Seven of Wands is also all about defending your title and position and proving your self-worth, as other opponents are often waiting to take your position and place in life by whatever underhanded means they can conjure up.

The Seven of Wands symbolises asserting your rights to be territorial if you are under attack and to rightfully stand for your deserved position in life.

This card is about the importance of cleverly warding off unnecessary harassers who are seeking an angle to one-up you.

KEYWORDS

UPRIGHT

- Challenges
- Competition
- Self-protection
- Perseverance
- Assertiveness
- Self-defence
- Stamina
- Territorial
- Standing up for yourself
- Strong will under attack
- Fully guarded

REVERSED

- Exhaustion
- Defeat
- Giving up
- Overwhelmed
- Surrender
- Yielding
- Lacking self-belief

EIGHT OF WANDS

EIGHT OF WANDS

The Eight of Wands shows eight wands taking off into the sky in full flight. All the wands are aligned and parallel, which indicates that all of the components involved in action are now aligned and any interference or unnecessary obstacles/complications have been attended to.

Behind the Eight of Wands is a lush, natural scene with green fields and trees, symbolising that the timing is ripe and ready.

The sky is calm and clear of bad weather; this, too, represents the timing is now perfect.

Beneath the flying Eight of Wands is a small blazing camp fire. This symbolises your energy tank and reserves are now also fully prepared for action and swift communication.

The Eight of Wands is all about everything being aligned for a swift change of pace so real momentum can seriously begin.

All of the past difficulties the Seven of Wands presented are now behind the person involved here. The absolute worst is over. Action and communication are what is needed.

The Eight of Wands is here to tell you that aspects of your life are now ready to trailblaze ahead.

Whatever you focus on will successfully take off, and real results will manifest.

KEYWORDS

UPRIGHT

- Communication
- Fast paced
- Movement
- Action
- Air travel
- Speed
- Quick decisions
- Being prepared
- Gaining momentum
- Sudden changes
- Alignment

REVERSED

- Delays
- Resisting change
- Not aligned
- Frustrations
- Losing momentum
- Waiting
- Slowness
- Being unprepared

NINE OF WANDS

The Nine of Wands shows a totally drained, injured man with his head bandaged up, which symbolises he is mentally, physically and emotionally drained and out of steam.

He leans on one of his nine wands for support. The other eight wands he strategically aligns for self-defence and protection. The wand he leans on represents his own will to stand till the end. The other eight wands represent the extra support systems he has aligned for himself.

The Nine of Wands man is completely worn out. He still stands ready and is bearing the raw battle scars. He tentatively awaits more possible battles while hoping it has ended. He is barely standing and needs to rest as he is so damaged and injured. He witnessed all the damage that unfolded from all sides involved. He processes this as he stands till the end.

KEYWORDS

UPRIGHT

- Resilience
- Courage
- Solid defence
- Healthy boundaries
- Grit
- Close to success
- Wounded
- Holding on
- Last stand
- Fatigued

REVERSED

- Overwhelmed
- Completely drained of energy
- Paranoid
- Refusing to compromise
- Stubborn

TEN OF WANDS

The Ten of Wands shows a strong yet tired man carrying ten wands on his shoulders and back.

The weary man carries his heavy load up a very steep hill. He is fully focused and pushing with every ounce of willpower and brute strength to drudge onwards and upwards to fulfil his goal. He knows his goal and exactly what must be done to achieve this. The path is difficult, lonesome and extremely tiring but his task must be completed.

The Ten of Wands man knows clearly where, why, when, what, who and how to achieve his destination. All of his actions, thoughts and willpower are based on carrying the necessary load to fulfil this goal to succeed. His exhaustion is no excuse to give up.

He will persevere through all the adversity, turmoil, duties, struggles and sufferings. He knows he has no other choice but to achieve what he must. He is aware he has done the hardest part and he is near the end of his struggles.

He knows everyone has a heavy cross they will one day have to bear. He is carrying his own cross and he can see his goal. The house on the far distant hill is his symbolic goal of success.

KEYWORDS

UPRIGHT
- Burdens
- Extra responsibilities
- Drudgery
- Hard work
- Stress
- Obligations
- Uphill struggles
- End in sight
- Burning out
- Heavy problems
- Lack of fun
- Having a strong backbone
- Fulfilling duties
- Perseverance

REVERSED
- Releasing burdens
- Breaking due to excessive stress
- Failure to complete workload
- Nervous breakdown
- Collapse
- Fallen apart
- Abandoning responsibilities

PAGE OF WANDS

The Page of Wands shows a young male casually and confidently standing while leaning on his staff/wand. His staff/wand has some small green leaves sprouting from it.

The Page of Wands is dressed in a bright yellow tunic with an ouroboros snake eating its tail displayed on it. This is symbolic of his natural and gifted ability to imaginatively transform small ideas into big ones with excitement and drive. He has the gift of the gab to persuade anybody, which can be a good or a bad thing depending on what he is driven towards.

The yellow tunic is representational of his solar plexus chakra, which is fully activated and energised. His smarts come from his finely tuned gut instinct.

He is fast thinking, talented and swift at processing a diverse range of information, but he is still youthful and may not always focus on what is the wisest thing.

The green sprouts on his staff/wand are indicating the many new inspirational ideas he has yet taken action towards.

The Page of Wands is youthful, full of curiosity and very adventurous. He does not always play by the rules but is lovable and charming.

The background is barren, which symbolises his natural ability to find potential where others do not see anything. The Page of Wands can make anything happen. He is so uplifting, charming, persuasive and full of great ideas.

KEYWORDS

UPRIGHT

- Adaptable
- Convincing
- Potential
- Great ideas
- Free spirit
- Extroverted
- Charming
- Lovable rogue
- Self-assured
- Talented
- Excited

REVERSED

- Lacking ideas
- Tantrums
- Boring
- Immaturity
- Self-limiting beliefs
- Casual
- Unreliable

KNIGHT OF WANDS

The Knight of Wands sits on his horse in full armour. He wears a yellow free-flowing robe, which indicates his gut instinct and free-spirited energy. The Knight of Wands is ready to charge his way ahead.

His helmet has long, free-flowing red tassels on top to reveal his energised passion and vigour for what he feels strongly about.

His horse rises on his hind legs, while also being poised and prepared for action.

The Knight of Wands holds a large, flamed wand in his right hand. This is representational of the zealous fervour that is sparked, fully activated and ready to charge ahead.

The Knight of Wands feels confident, self-assured, enthusiastic and fully driven to go full steam ahead.

He is rebellious in nature, revolutionary in spirit, open-minded and a free thinker. This may or may not be a good thing; it all depends on where his passions lie and why.

The Knight of Wands is caring and has a big open heart, but he can turn on anyone who attempts to tame him or corner him into a position he does not wish to be in.

KEYWORDS

UPRIGHT
- Passionate
- Revolutionary
- Fervour
- Adventurous
- Visceral
- Impulsive
- Gut instinct
- Free spirit
- Swift action
- Charming
- Inspired
- Zealous
- Energetic

REVERSED
- Volatile
- Reckless
- Scattered energy
- Delays
- Frustrations
- Uninspired
- Stuck
- Dispassionate

QUEEN OF WANDS

The Queen of Wands sits confidently on her blue throne, which has two lions crested on the top. These lions represent her leadership bloodlines.

The Queen of Wands is highly independent. She holds a wand in one hand and a sunflower in her other hand. The wand represents her passionate and lively self while the sunflower represents her fertility, satisfaction and happiness with her life.

She is bold, fun loving, flirtatious, a bit cheeky and definitely sassy in her ways. The Queen of Wands is never a shrinking violet. She is extroverted and confident and expects to be heard and seen. Shy she is not.

The Queen of Wands enjoys taking the lead and making a statement that demands attention. Her red gown is representational of her fiery, fearless, passionate, sexy and bold self. She is a straight shooter and enjoys being so. What you see is what you get, and if people do not like what they see she has no issue with that. She is very much in touch with her shadow self and is a force to be reckoned with.

The Queen of Wands holds a powerful presence. Her feisty and spirited ways naturally demand attention. She is very friendly, extremely giving and charming but she will not be pushed around. She knows who she is and she wears this with pride. Her strong mind and independent way of thinking have given her strong and clear boundaries and her boundaries empower her even more.

KEYWORDS

UPRIGHT
- Self-assured
- Charismatic
- Sassy
- Extrovert
- Confident
- Popular
- Sexy
- Assertive
- Outgoing
- Passionate
- Vivacious

REVERSED
- Attention seeking
- Demanding
- Selfish
- Bossy
- Introvert
- Temperamental
- Uses sex as a weapon
- Vengeful

KING OF WANDS

The King of Wands comfortably sits on his throne with the harsh desert landscape surrounding him. The harsh landscape is symbolic of the King of Wands' ability to be highly driven, confident, capable, strong and motivated, even when hardships are thrown at him.

The King of Wands' throne has a lion's head image on the top. The lion's head symbolises the King of Wands' natural fearlessness, powerful presence and his effective ability to lead others through anything.

The King of Wands holds a flaming torch/wand with his right hand that represents his fiery, passionate and free-spirited nature that does not back down.

He wears a leopard-skin coat that is reflective of his raw, free-spirited and swift ways to get things done with charm, talent and confidence. The King of Wands adorns headwear that is dominated by the colour red to represent his passion and power. The yellow triangle with a red centre on the front of his headwear signifies his intelligence and heartfelt passion. The triangle is representational of his fire sign and fiery nature. On the very top of his headwear hides an ouroboros, which is symbolic of his infinite capacity and extensive drive to boldly push through all obstacles.

The giant goanna pet next to his feet represents his strong exterior and fighting spirit, always ready to go the distance.

The King of Wands is funny, charming, confident and highly energetic. He is great with all types of people and very adaptable. He values freedom, self-expression and is highly independent. He is action oriented and efficient and despises victimhood and neediness. The King of Wands is, however, very supportive to those who help themselves.

He is as proud as a lion, swift as a leopard, resilient as a goanna and protective to the end to all he loves and respects.

KEYWORDS

UPRIGHT
- Natural-born leader
- Bold
- Confident
- Energetic
- Visionary
- Proud
- Passionate
- Fearlessness
- Highly motivated
- Self-driven
- Free thinker
- Action oriented

REVERSED
- Ineffective
- Domineering
- Cruel
- Short temper
- Vicious
- Weak leader
- Forceful

ACE OF SWORDS

ACE OF SWORDS

The Ace of Swords displays a giant hand holding a sword that has a glorious, golden crown of jewels and an all-seeing third eye haloed above it.

Ironically, the hand comes out from a cloud that is outside the global bubble the hand is supposedly inside. Large green lush vines drape out of the golden crown of jewels, surrounding the sword.

The sword pierces right through the border of the spherical bubble, resembling earth, and juts out into the eternal cosmic truth of even more life.

The golden crown is symbolic of cosmic connected consciousness. The third eye represents the dimensional eye of perceptual awareness that is logical and coherent but far more expanded in understanding matters. The vines draping out of the cup are symbolic of the knowledge of life. The cloud the hand comes from represents intellectual sparks of genius that seemingly come from nowhere. The hand is symbolic like all ace cards of new assistance.

The Ace of Swords has triumphed and completely broken through the hidden membrane of higher intelligence and comprehensive awareness, of multidimensional levels simultaneously.

The Ace of Swords embodies swift insight beyond regurgitated and trained levels of knowledge. The Ace of Swords has entered into the very beginning phases of specialised knowledge.

KEYWORDS

UPRIGHT
- Initiation
- Breakthrough
- Crystalised intelligence
- Authority
- New beginnings
- Intensity
- Victory
- Realised truth
- Inventors
- Cosmic consciousness
- Success
- Total coherence
- Effective communication

REVERSED
- Re-thinking ideas
- Clouded judgement
- Mental fogginess
- Miscommunication
- Confusion
- Believing half truths
- Incoherent thinking

TWO OF SWORDS

TWO OF SWORDS

The Two of Swords shows a person in a basic black robe with a sack tied firmly over their head.

The two swords the person holds across their chest symbolise the two options they have available.

The person sits on a big box on the ground with clouds on it in front of a beach scene with the same clouds behind them.

The bag over the person's head is symbolic of the inner dark world they are trapped in. This dark inner world is paralysing for it reveals an information overload of both of the options available. While knowing full well neither option is truly where this person wants to go, do or be.

The Two of Swords person is metaphorically stuck between a rock and a hard place and is forced to choose one or the other.

The black gown they wear is symbolic of their emotional space, which is dark for they feel cornered to make a decision.

The person sits very still, perfectly balanced, listening to and absorbing the serene vibrations of the gentle waters rolling in and out. They are weighing up all of their options from both sides, the pros and cons of both. Wanting neither option (or maybe wanting both without relinquishing the other) yet knowing a decision must be made.

The two unbeknown feathers floating above the person's bagged head are symbolic of the individual's blindness to what other choices they also have but have yet to recognise.

The Two of Swords is still deciding based on what they are able to perceive at this stage.

KEYWORDS

UPRIGHT

- Difficult decision
- Painful choices
- Stalemate
- Pros and cons
- No right choice
- Damned if you do, damned if you don't
- Information overload
- Stuck in the middle
- Checkmate
- Standstill
- Wanting your cake and eating it
- Sitting on the fence
- Torn between two lovers

REVERSED

- Seeing another way out
- Truth revealed
- Abandoning all available options
- Wild card
- Not deciding
- Transcending beyond given options
- Success totally against all odds

THREE OF SWORDS

THREE OF SWORDS

The Three of Swords is iconic and, sadly, painfully obvious.

The Three of Swords depicts a giant heart floating alone in the miserable rain-crying sky. The only thing holding it somewhat together are the two red and blue giant blood vessels on either side of it, desperately trying to pump vital blood through the vulnerable bleeding, broken, seriously damaged heart.

This heart has three different swords pierced right through it like it is a piece of meat. There are bandages tied around the heart trying desperately to mend it. Blood is seeping out of the heart while bandage tape is put on in the hope of stopping it.

The red and blue veins are pulsating and attempting to sustain the heart, but this heart is broken and in terrible pain.

The heart is the vital organ that keeps us physically alive. It is also where we store our warmth, connection, emotions and feelings.

The Three of Swords is the symbol for complete emotional heartbreak. However it happened, the heart is spiritually bleeding apart inside and in total grief, loss and sadness. Immense, cruel, emotional suffering is being experienced.

The Three of Swords: the card nobody ever wants to experience.

KEYWORDS

UPRIGHT
- Broken heart
- Sorrow
- Trauma
- Hurting inside
- Depression
- Sadness
- Tears
- Disillusioned
- Loss
- Grief
- Emotional pain
- Heartache
- Alienation
- Closed-off heart chakra
- Separation

REVERSED
- Releasing pain
- Optimism
- Hope
- Forgiveness
- Healing
- Repressed emotions
- Opening-up heart chakra

FOUR OF SWORDS

FOUR OF SWORDS

The Four of Swords image shows a man lying down, eyes closed, resting or sleeping on a bed.

The man lies on the bed gently holding his sword, which lies over his bare chest and heart as he serenely drifts away.

It appears the man has found a place of sanctuary to rest his weary body, heart and mind. He is in real need of recuperation. What happened previously we do not know.

Behind the sleeping man we see a tapestry hanging on the rear wall to the left that displays three swords standing parallel and downwards decorated with flowering vines. We do know the Three of Swords is the tarot card of heartbreak but this image is the Four of Swords.

On the back wall to the right we see a beautiful circular stained glass window that reveals an image of a lady and small child. The two have halos, indicating maybe he is recuperating in a holy temple, or is this just symbolic of what is going on inside his own temple within and could the lady and child be his holy connection? Whatever the real story, the man is resting and in need of solitude and sleep.

The Four of Swords is the card for finding sanctuary, to get much-needed solitude, rest, sleep and rejuvenation.

UPRIGHT

- Rest
- Time out
- Meditation
- Relaxation
- Rejuvenation
- Needing solitude
- Regrouping
- Having faith
- Dreaming
- Planning

REVERSED

- Exhaustion
- Hospitalisation
- Re-entering the world
- Awakening from a slumber
- Burnt out
- Illness
- Restlessness
- Isolation

FIVE OF SWORDS

In the Five of Swords, a conceited-looking gentleman takes front stage of the image while he stands holding three of the five swords, looking sly and rather pleased with himself.

In the far distance we see two deflated, possibly humiliated gentlemen slowly, silently and humbly retreating into the woods.

Two of the five swords lay crossed on the ground in between both oppositional sides. This highly suggests the two walking away, slouched and quiet, were indeed defeated – so defeated it was not even worth taking the two remaining swords. Clearly the conflict involved more than swords to the losers. Either way the happy gentleman who won has his three swords.

The two gentlemen walking away have been reproached or possibly bribed somehow. The true extent of conflict we will never really know. If it was fair or not we can only assume.

Whatever the win, it does seem to have a bittersweet feel to it.

The Five of Swords is symbolic of what is more important: winning at all costs to appear victorious so the other side loses at all costs too, or negotiating the conflicted situation and seeking a compromise and healthy resolution for all involved.

KEYWORDS

UPRIGHT

- Bittersweet
- Winning at all costs
- Competition
- Losing friendships
- Hostility
- Disputes
- Unresolved conflicts
- Disagreements
- Defeated
- Having to be right all the time
- Uncompromising
- Bribery
- Always wanting to be the top dog
- Bullying

REVERSED

- Compromising
- Remorse
- Regret
- Humility
- Forgiveness
- Making amends
- Resolving conflicts

SIX OF SWORDS

SIX OF SWORDS

The Six of Swords shows a woman and small child in a boat being rowed by a man through choppy waters. The man is taking them towards safe lands on the horizon. The woman and child huddle together under blankets.

The scene strongly indicates they are fleeing from something out of necessity. The sadness from the blanketed woman and child's faces reveals this escape has not been emotionally easy or pleasant in any way whatsoever. The man rowing the boat looks fiercely protective and determined to make it to dry land.

The woman and child symbolise the vulnerability from sadness and loss that must be faced in order to truly overcome previous hardship.

The man rowing the boat symbolises the strength of the mind and sheer willpower required to do exactly what must be done and take all knocks fair and square like an adult.

The entire scene on the Six of Swords is about finally learning extremely hard lessons from the past, once and for all, so the lesson is never repeated.

The six swords standing upright in the boat are representational of the mind's strength to get through it to the end, standing tall, knowing you had the mental and psychological tenacity to overcome all preceding obstacles.

The red ribbon tied to one of the standing swords represents the internal resources and power within to save yourself.

The Six of Swords is symbolic of transitioning by learning lessons. It is representational of acquiring personal rites of passage from psychological childhood nonsense into authentic and integrated adult thinking and being.

KEYWORDS

UPRIGHT

- Transition
- Calm after the storm
- Hard lessons learned
- Rites of passage
- Overcoming hardship
- Escaping the worst
- Relief
- Releasing outdated baggage
- Healthy departure
- Finished business
- Matters settled
- Letting go of what no longer serves your higher good
- Tying up loose ends

REVERSED

- Resistance to change
- Self-denial
- Trapped
- Unfinished business
- Not learning your lesson
- Running away from your problems
- Stuck in the past
- Returning to trouble

SEVEN OF SWORDS

The Seven of Swords shows a cloaked and concealed person tiptoeing away in the quiet of the night, carrying five swords and leaving two swords where they belong.

The Seven of Swords person discreetly looks over their shoulder as they slip away from what appears to be a large group of camps. Clearly the people at the camp site are all asleep.

The thief appears to be very proficient in the sly arts of disguise and getting away with something unnoticed. They appear to be experienced and confident in going under the radar.

However, unbeknown to the masqueraded looter, we see a small, unrecognisable creature lurking behind some rocks observing the entire scene being played out.

The bandit represents a secretive, strategic person not showing all of their cards. The image suggests the motive is for illicit reasons, but context is everything.

Whatever is being hidden and done under the radar, the small hiding creature knows who the underhanded culprit is. The hidden creature is symbolic of the individual's lurking conscience.

KEYWORDS

UPRIGHT

- Betrayal
- Deception
- Sneakiness
- Resourceful
- Getting away with something
- Acting strategically
- Trickery
- Blindsided
- Hoodwinked
- Cunning
- Underhanded
- Half truths
- Lies
- Masquerading as a friend
- Mental manipulation
- Covert
- Disclosure

REVERSED

- Overt
- Open
- Confession
- Truth revealed
- Revelation
- Exposure
- Admission
- Sincere apology
- Regret
- Healthy confidentiality

EIGHT OF SWORDS

The Eight of Swords shows a blindfolded woman bound with a thin rope. She stands alone in a barren place with some shallow puddles around her. Eight black birds fly in the sky in the far distance.

The puddles represent the small issues she believes are insurmountable. The black birds represent her higher mind waiting to take charge.

Eight massive swords pierced into the dirt surround her. At first glance, it appears the woman is fully trapped. However, the thin rope she is tied up with could easily be undone if she persevered and made the effort to take control of the situation. She could then remove her blindfold and assess the situation correctly.

The entire image is symbolic of a person who is self-imprisoning themselves by not taking control of a situation to see what is really going on. The woman, blindfolded and bound, represents a person stuck in a victimised, self-limiting mindset. All is not nearly as bad as it initially appears: the dilemma can be resolved if she chooses to face her fears and not be led by an imagined situation of learned helplessness.

If she chose to release her negative self-talk within she would see the eight massive swords surrounding her are only symbolic, self-defeating, fear-based mental props she can easily release herself from if she faces her fears.

KEYWORDS

UPRIGHT

- Self-imposed restrictions
- Inner critic
- Victim mentality
- Self-doubt
- Feeling trapped and imprisoned mentally
- Anxiety
- Feeling paralysed
- Feeling pressured
- Learned helplessness
- Dilemma
- Not seeing a way out
- Backed into a corner

REVERSED

- Facing fears
- Conquering your own demons
- Survivor
- Taking back control
- Empowered
- Integrating shadow self
- Shifting into healthy perspectives
- Releasing imagined boogey men

NINE OF SWORDS

NINE OF SWORDS

The Nine of Swords shows a woman sitting in her bed late at night and alone. She looks deeply distressed as she cups her face in her hands.

The Nine of Swords woman may have awakened from a terrifying nightmare or is suffering unbearable insomnia through worry and anxiety. Either way, she is going through a private experience that is despairing, isolating and deeply unpleasant.

Above and around her hang nine swords in mid-air with sharp points directed towards her head. To add to this, the nine swords all have red blood dripping from them that symbolise the piercing mental suffering she is enduring. The dripping blood emphasises the degree of mental pain and despair she is experiencing.

The woman has a very heavy heart, and is defeated and seriously burdened by whatever is going through her mind.

Whether the actual issues in her mind are valid or not, she is suffering total mental anguish. The woman may merely be catastrophising some concern to be far worse than it actually is and cognitive distortion has consumed her thoughts, or her anguish is fully justified.

No matter what, she is mentally agonising.

KEYWORDS

UPRIGHT

- Worry
- Nightmares
- Insomnia
- Despair
- Agonise
- Catastrophise
- Isolation
- Overwhelmed
- Mental health issues
- Stress
- Remorse
- Deep unhappiness
- Burdened
- Migraines
- Not coping

REVERSED

- Releasing worries
- Learning to cope
- Finding help
- Recovering from mental health issues
- Developing inner peace
- Acceptance
- Finally feeling rested

TEN OF SWORDS

The Ten of Swords shows what appears to be a dead or dying man. He is lying face down on a beach with ten long swords pierced through his bleeding back.

The background ocean scene is peaceful, relaxed and calm while the image of the man is confronting, eerie and despairingly negative. The worst and most painful damage and harm has been done. The final and last nail in the coffin has happened.

The Ten of Swords is the card that represents major, disastrous endings. The Ten of Swords image also suggests the final crisis into complete collapse was most likely not foreseen.

Enemies for whatever reason wreak all through the Ten of Swords image. Collapse, breakdown and complete ruin have happened, and people have been seriously hurt.

There has clearly been a serious betrayal of some description. Everything has come to an excruciating and quiet dead end and all that remains is silence and blood. The blood symbolises the suffering and pain that has been endured. Everything has been shot down, metaphorically speaking.

On a slightly more positive note, the Ten of Swords does imply the worst is now behind you. All endings, no matter how painful, always bring new opportunities when the time is ripe.

As unpleasant as the Ten of Swords is, sometimes certain collapses are necessary so actual renewal and healing can begin in a better way than before.

KEYWORDS

UPRIGHT

- Enemies
- Painful endings
- Nervous breakdown
- Ruin
- Bitterness
- Despair
- Crisis
- Deep wounds
- Dead end
- Collapse
- Inability to cope
- Rock bottom

REVERSED

- Recovery from loss or illness
- Regeneration
- Resisting the inevitable end
- Situation improving
- Survival
- Lesson learned
- Healing

PAGE OF SWORDS

PAGE OF SWORDS

The Page of Swords shows a youthful male standing outside and holding his sword in his hand.

His sword leans to his left while the young page's body is turning more to his right. This reveals he is vigilant, curious and alert and ready to go straight to wherever his curiosity and hunch take him.

The Page of Swords wears a small black mask around his eyes, which indicates that he is the type of person who likes to learn, gather information and delve. If, however, he is not careful, his curious, driven nature can tempt him into spying.

The clouds in the sky and tree blowing in the far distance show it is windy, as does his flowing red cape and hair. This symbolises the Page of Swords' swift and very fast-moving mental capacity to gather and process information.

The Page of Swords is engaging and very young at heart and will never intentionally harm others.

The Page of Swords does, however, have to harness his swift, curious and talented mind so he does not get tempted into a useless, petty, gossipy gathering of energy-wasting information.

The Page of Swords is chatty, youthful, witty and very likeable to everyone who knows him. Oddly, though, because the Page of Swords possesses such a sharp, inquisitive mind he mostly prefers to be a bit of a loner.

KNIGHT OF SWORDS

KNIGHT OF SWORDS

The Knight of Swords depicts a fully armoured knight charging ahead through the sky on her grey winged horse.

She raises her sword in the air and appears to be yelling 'Charge!' as she soars forward through the sky.

She is in battle mode and nothing will stop her.

The Knight of Swords is symbolic of a sharp-minded, fast-thinking person who is fully focused, courageous and even rebellious.

The yellow sky is symbolic of her intellect. The flying horse is representational of her swiftness and ability to be efficient and not a time waster.

The Knight of Swords is representational of a person who is daring, a fast thinker, a fast talker and fast in actioning whatever it is that must be done.

The Knight of Swords is usually all about a person who is quick and/or a witty type in personality. They are always fiercely sharp of mind and very direct and focused. The Knight of Swords does not get distracted and aims directly forward and towards their goal or outcome. Dawdling and time wasting is never on the agenda for the Knight of Swords.

KEYWORDS

UPRIGHT
- Daring
- Ambitious
- Driven
- Efficient
- Seizes the moment
- Fully charged
- Assertive
- Focused
- Talkative
- Risk taker
- Swift
- Fast thinking
- Action oriented
- Rebellious

REVERSED
- Bully
- Dilly-dally
- Vicious
- Arrogant
- Compliant
- Tactless
- Unfocused
- Easily distracted

QUEEN OF SWORDS

The Queen of Swords sits on her soft feminine throne, indicating that beneath her cool, stern appearance there is a softer side seated in her.

The Queen of Swords holds her sharp blade to the sky to symbolise her high level of knowledge and her sharp intelligence.

Her hand is bleeding from the sword. This reveals the principled pains she is committed to to maintain her clear set of personal boundaries and self-agency.

Her pastel pink, gold and baby blue floral-designed throne indicates her sophisticated tastes for refinement and elegance.

The queen's throne is placed upon a solid, cold slab of concrete, which reveals her unwavering and unapologetic means to an end.

She is situated high up in the isolated green mountains. This symbolises her high level of independence and her unbeatable levels of intelligence.

The Queen of Swords stands for herself and she is incredibly perceptive.

Unconventional is the Queen of Swords' style. She follows her own individuality, even quirkiness. She thinks for herself as her mental ability to problem solve is super sharp and excellent.

The Queen of Swords can be perceived as being stern, even emotionless. However, she is a highly principled woman who is honest and very candid.

Behind the Queen of Swords' cold and sophisticated appearance is an empathic, self-reliant woman who assesses everything with crystal clarity.

The Queen of Swords is the seeker of truth. She breaks down all factual and seemingly factual information before ever conclusively deciding anything.

KEYWORDS

UPRIGHT

- Sophisticated
- Clear boundaries
- Honest
- Quirky
- Strong-minded
- Objective
- Fair
- Unbiased judgement
- Constructive criticism
- Problem solver
- Perceptive
- Direct communication
- Open-minded
- Sceptical

REVERSED

- Narrow-minded
- Cold hearted
- Bitchy
- Spiteful
- Unforgiving
- Easily influenced
- Pessimistic

KING OF SWORDS

The King of Swords sits cross-legged on his leather throne inside his dark castle, holding his sword in the air and with his floating golden crown around his sword.

He is the cool, calm and rational voice of reason.

The King of Swords exudes profoundly high levels of intelligence and acute degrees of intellectual power. He is prone to being aloof and distant; however, he is articulate, diplomatic, precise and extremely eloquent in his manners and prowess of delivering information.

He seeks nothing but the cold-hearted truth of matters and uses his brilliant mind to do so.

The King of Swords does not display high levels of emotion or even affection. Even though he is undemonstrative and reserved in nature he is sincere and loyal to those he cares for. He is always a man of high integrity.

The King of Swords is ruled by his head. The golden crown around his sword is symbolic of this truth. He is razor sharp, discerning, astute, decisive and detached.

This highly educated king values clarity of thought and coherence in comprehending. He is not easily fooled by any stretch of the measure. His quietness is due to his fast and skilful mental processing abilities. He is respected by all.

KEYWORDS

UPRIGHT
- Educated
- Intellect
- Articulate
- Eloquent
- Truth
- Integrity
- Knowledgeable
- Stern
- Logical
- Manners
- Polite
- High standards
- Gentlemanly
- Aloof

REVERSED
- Dictator
- Ruthless
- Dishonest
- Oppressive
- Cruel
- Inhumane
- Rude

ABOUT THE AUTHOR AND ILLUSTRATOR

Lisa Porter is a self-taught artist/illustrator who was born and raised in Northampton, a tiny rural town in the isolated wheat-belt area of Western Australia. She has been drawing since she was old enough to pick up a crayon.

Her first inspirations came from old, handed-down, hard-cover children's picture books that were illustrated with awe-inspiring cyclops, monsters and giants. Her older sibling's comics were also a childhood source of visual inspiration for her.

During the 1990s she was a popular freelance caricature artist and court-hearing illustrator for a newspaper.

Esoteric literature has been an ongoing fascination her entire adult life. The study of ancient pagan mysticism, mythology, archetypal allegories, ufology and xenology are a constant preoccupation of interest for her. She is deeply interested in the relationship of the living occult's timeless narratives, which are intrinsically connected to the psychology of the human mind, body and soul. Her love of creating art has always been a massive part of her life. The human subject and all the extended character variables have been a never-ending creative passion of hers.